Journey to My Daughter

Dina,

Thank you.

I hope you enjoy

Jennifer Rose Ash

Journey to My Daughter

A Memoir about Adoption and Self-Discovery

Jennifer Rose Asher

New Degree Press

Copyright © 2021 Jennifer Rose Asher

Journey to My Daughter

A Memoir about Adoption and Self-Discovery

ISBN   978-1-63730-694-9   *Paperback*

978-1-63730-784-7   *Kindle Ebook*

979-8-88504-022-8   *Ebook*

*I dedicate this book to the three amazing
humans who have made me a mother:
Hilary, Jamie, and Reese.
I hope you will read this and understand
how far I would go for any of you.*

Contents

Author's Note

———

This book is my adoption story, but it is much more than that. It is also the story of how I discovered what is important in life and how I learned to trust the universe.

I grew up believing if I ever wanted to have a child, I would just decide to have one. Then nine short months later, I would have a baby. I think many little girls grow up with this same line of thinking. I don't know why very little is taught about infertility and miscarriage when we take health class, but it would have been nice to have some warning.

It seems to me that no one tells most daughters it is not always simple to just have a child once they are married and make the decision it is time to start a family. Few people share stories of infertility and miscarriage, especially beyond a small group of close friends. Even the struggles and difficulties involved in adopting a child are not often discussed or elaborated upon.

My husband and I came to the decision that it was time for us to start a family, and I was truly shocked when our child didn't just appear without incident nine months later. I experienced miscarriages followed by failed adoption attempts and finally the successful adoption of a beautiful baby girl.

I had many adventures along the way before finding my first child, including multiple heartbreaks, lots of tears, and even a few laughs. I learned a lot about things I never thought I would learn, such as the risks of losing pregnancies and what the progression and growth of a fetus should look like. I studied the cultures of many countries I previously knew little about and even traveled to see a country and culture I never would have thought I would be able to see for myself. I became intimately acquainted with all of the paperwork required for adoptions from several different countries and eventually what is required to adopt domestically within the United States. I got to know how laws and requirements differ for adopting from multiple countries and from different states within our own country.

I also discovered a lot about myself and my husband as well as how we would weather many types of crises and obstacles. I learned I am tougher than I thought, and there are times to push but other times when kindness and grace is required. I learned I can depend on myself, even when the going gets tough, but I can also rely on my family and friends to lend a hand and make things easier when needed.

I've made friends from all over the world on this journey. I discovered how important it is to know the right people and how fortunate it can be when they enter my life just when they are needed.

I laughed, I cried, and now I've written a book!

This is the memoir of how I remember the journey. At times I changed or omitted names of people when I wasn't sure if they would want readers to recognize them. When I didn't remember exact details and dialogue, I did my best to recreate them in the spirit in which they occurred.

I experienced a lot of things for which I never learned the outcome—mysteries I never solved and which seem like loose ends, even to me. I did my best to resolve confusion for the reader whenever possible but did not want to presume resolution when I never got actual clarification or understanding of puzzling events I observed or experienced. I can guess about what I think probably happened through conjecture and by putting things together in my head, but when I didn't have the actual facts, I left conclusions for readers to decide for themselves.

I now believe things are meant to happen in their own way and in their own time. I think often, if not always, specific children are meant to be brought into their specific family. They may travel to their families through traditional birth or with the help of fertility treatments, surrogacy, or adoption. This journey to find my daughter taught me this. I am still regularly reminded that my daughter is special and unique. She was truly meant to be in *our* family.

I needed to follow signs given by the universe to find my unique child. It was imperative that I allowed everything to happen as it was supposed to. Signs popped up along the way, directing me, but I was not always wise enough to follow them. The direction I needed to move stayed the same—whether I listened or not—and when I veered off course, a new signal would guide me back on track.

As a simple example, when I first decided to adopt a child, I thought she would be Chinese. I knew several families who had adopted daughters from China. I really wanted a girl and knew so many girls were available for adoption in China, so I just fixated on that particular country and held tightly to it. An even bigger priority (bigger than the importance of the baby's gender) for me was timeline and completing the adoption process as quickly as possible. I had made this preference my very most important factor in selecting an agency or program. As I researched agencies with China adoption programs, they were all quoting very long wait times, which should have been a sign that this was not the right country for me to adopt from since the timeline was the most important aspect of the adoption for me. I persisted well beyond a reasonable time, holding on to this plan to go to China and calling every agency I could find with a China program who literally all said the same thing about wait times. Instead of shifting my investigation of adoption programs in a different direction or at least widening it to include other options, I kept searching for the one magic agency that could get me a Chinese baby in a time frame I now know is not reasonable for that country.

Eventually, I was basically hit over the head by my friend, Micki, the representative from an agency who worked with both China and Vietnam. She explained very explicitly that the process in China goes through the central government and will have the same wait time regardless of agency. She compared it directly with their program in Vietnam, illustrating the process in Vietnam where each province made their own adoption rules. Because of this, it is possible to "shop" different orphanages based upon the province where they are located, thus choosing a specific process that can be completed more quickly. I finally saw the fork in the road and was able to choose the Vietnamese path that clearly matched my own priorities, making my uphill battle take a turn for the better.

I believe these signs direct us not only to our children but throughout our lives, toward our destiny. We can choose to follow the signs or not, but they will only reappear in new forms to help steer us where we need to go. Listening to these advising guides and following more closely to their suggestions has brought me increased peace and joy beyond what I could have expected.

I hope this story can help future parents listen to their guides.

I want people, especially women, to know they are not alone if they experience miscarriage, or infertility, or failed adoption. I pray they can come to accept that these experiences, although devastating, do not diminish them as women or as human beings. It is possible to find a silver lining in these miserable storm clouds, and it is important not to allow them to cast a dark cloud over the rest of life.

On the surface, I may educate readers about the logistics and possible pitfalls in the adoption process; I elaborate on the details of the paperwork and steps required to adopt a child. I shine a light on some of the roadblocks that can pop up on the way to finalizing an adoption.

For readers who may adopt, as well as those who never will, I hope reading my story will inspire hope, courage, and strength for anyone embarking on their own journey.

I originally wrote this story several years ago because I wanted to record the events before I forgot what happened. I wanted my daughter, Hilary, to know how our paths came together and how hard we worked to find her.

I decided to share the story of this journey with the world in the hope that it will help other people. I wish that my readers will enjoy the story and that some may find solace, hope, and faith in it.

Although families touched by adoption will be drawn to this book, and indeed it was initially directed at those readers, I now believe this story can inspire a much larger audience. I have tried to illustrate the types of patterns that at first just cause frustration but in retrospect may be forces guiding us in a different direction. I would love for readers facing adversity in challenging and unpredictable or uncertain times to use these examples to help guide their own journey in a way that will be most satisfying and successful for them.

If I am able to help even one other person trust the universe, find patience to allow life to fall into place, make an adoption process more tolerable, or even just bring a smile to a reader's face, the hours I have spent writing and editing have been very worthwhile.

I have been so blessed. I not only have my perfect daughter but two perfect sons as well as the husband I believe was meant for me. I am very excited to share my adoption story and bring you along with me on this journey. Welcome!

*The universe conspires to reveal the truth
and to make your path easy
if you have the courage to follow the signs.*

—*AUTHOR: LISA UNGER*

Chapter 1

No Kids, Just Horses

For the first twenty-nine years of my life, I was sure I would never have children. I did not think questioning this belief and simply opening my mind to the possibility of having a child of my own would change my life completely. This single thought led me on a journey literally to the other side of the earth and back, changing who I am and how I see the world for the rest of my life.

I never wanted to have any kids. I don't mean that I didn't really want them; I mean I actively, strongly, passionately, aggressively would fight for my right to *never* have children and would debate this point with any well-meaning friend, family member, or stranger who would dare to question my position.

I guess I should explain further why I felt so strongly about this. I was always a very outspoken and very strong-willed person, and even in childhood I had a great need to make any attitude or opinion concrete and definite. I often saw the world as clearly black or white, and it was easier for me to hold tightly to the extreme of my positions than to question them.

When I was a young child I didn't have a ton of friends, and I really didn't like playing the kinds of games most kids play. I didn't enjoy spending time outside, playing board games, or dressing dolls, and I absolutely hated any form of active game or sport. I saw other kids my age as immature and boring. In addition to my dislike for children in general, I also had two younger brothers. I was in constant competition with my brothers, and they did nothing to improve my opinion of younger kids.

As a teenager I could never relate to children who were younger than me. Babysitting was like torture. I found myself pretending to enjoy rocking a baby to sleep, trying to interact and relate with toddlers, or feigning interest in the games of grade school kids. I was miserable every time I needed money so desperately that I agreed to a Saturday night watching a neighbor's kids.

Although my opinions and preferences were close to set in stone once I identified them, I was a curious child from early on and gathered information hungrily about the world around me. My mother did her best to answer all of my endless questions, often too completely. She told me where babies come from at a very early age. I guess I must have asked about it, but I think I was only about five years old. Even though I was young, I have a very strong, almost visual memory of my mother's explanation of childbirth and my reactive feelings about it.

First she told me that being pregnant was like having an alien living inside you, and it was creepy and miserable not to have control of your own body for nine months. Then she described childbirth. She told me it was the most awful, dirty, painful event a woman could ever experience. Well, the impression *that* left on my mind was more than concrete. I could almost taste the excruciating physical pain and had no warm emotions regarding babies or young children to temper the mental picture of that pain. When combined with my disgust for all children younger than me, my mother's description left quite a strong negative impression of actually giving birth to a child, which remained burned in my consciousness for decades to come.

While other young girls dreamed of getting married and having kids, I dreamed about a future life of owning and riding horses every day. I have always had an almost irrational love for horses. I would say as strongly as I felt about disliking other children, I felt just as strongly in the opposite direction about these majestic animals. The fact that I believed I never wanted to have kids was simply a part of who I was, and this somehow innate attraction to horses was also an integral part of my self-image. When I was a child I would draw, sculpt, and read about horses. I don't really remember this as a childhood obsession, but I have seen the ancient evidence in my mother's collection of memorabilia.

While I can't explain or even remember this very early attraction to horses, I can clearly recall when I was a bit older the feeling of bliss I experienced whenever I was in the barn or anywhere near these amazing animals. Horses exude a feeling of silent strength. Just standing in a stall, they somehow seem wise and able to shoulder and withstand taking on all of my weight—not just physically, but also emotionally.

I felt then, and still feel, a wave of calm wash over me when I stand at the pasture fence or in the doorway of a stall, watching a pony lazily munch on hay or grass. Somehow, horses are able to absorb a huge amount of stress and tension, relieving me of that burden. I find their simple approach to life and strength of conviction incredibly soothing and reassuring.

When I have the privilege of riding a horse, even on a pony ride when I was little, the rhythm of their gait creates a form of meditation for me. From the first time I felt this motion, it made me feel powerful and free in a way that nothing else did, and I could not get enough of this feeling.

I didn't grow up in Texas or on a ranch with horses all around me. I lived in a fairly urban suburb of Chicago where there were no barns within about a half hour's drive, so I didn't ride when I was very young because I simply never had an opportunity. I was just somehow born with this desire to be near horses. I only actually saw horses at rare summer carnivals or if we saw horse-drawn carriage rides on a trip to the city. I was just innately drawn to these animals if I ran across them in person or even in books or movies.

It wasn't until I was almost in middle school when I had the opportunity to spend more than a random afternoon with horses. During the summers of my pre-teen years, my mother didn't want me in her hair, or watching TV, and she didn't care what it cost to keep me out of the house. She told me I was allowed to go to any summer camp I wanted, as long as I didn't stay home all summer. I did tons of research on my options and managed to find camps that offered as much time riding as possible.

I longed to have my own horse but knew that would simply never happen. During high school my parents allowed me to take riding lessons once a week during the school year for a while. However, they weren't happy about how far away the barn was, and I had to take a bus to get there. Riding is also a very expensive pastime, which definitely didn't help my case. At this time during the eighties, kids didn't automatically have sports or activities. My parents were not particularly supportive of my riding, and eventually the logistics became too difficult. So I gave it up.

By the time I went to college, I repressed my desire to be a barn rat, cleaning stalls and grooming horses all day. I decided instead to get married and become a successful businesswoman in the financial world. I started dating Marc, who is now my husband.

Marc was kind of geeky and interested in computers, with a college major of engineering physics. This was a stark contrast to the silly, fun-loving sorority girl I was at the time. However, he was also kind, loving, brilliant, fun to hang out with, and could definitely hold his own against me in a discussion. In appearance he could be my brother; we were both on the short side with a fairly average build and both had greenish-hazel eyes with light olive skin. Our hair belied the Jewish heritage we shared—thick, dark, and frizzy—and we both wore it in typical eighties styles. He had a mullet and I had thick bangs cut straight across my forehead. I thought he was pretty darn cute, and from the time we started dating neither of us ever really looked for anyone else.

I remember fairly early in our dating relationship expressing to him in no uncertain terms that children were not something that would ever be a part of my future. The look of surprise on his face was mixed with humor, and I could tell he didn't think this was an issue in our current situation.

"No!" I told him. "This is not funny. If you want to have kids, there's no point in going any further in this relationship." I made my point as clear as I could.

"I guess I always thought I'd have kids, but it's not a deal breaker or anything," he told me.

"Well, it is for me," I told him sternly.

Any prior visions of laughing rug rats must have diminished for Marc, since he continued dating me. In fact, he eventually married me and never asked me to reconsider my position.

Even as a young adult, children of any age continued to annoy me whenever I spent time with them, and I was glad I had absolutely no responsibility for them. They got on my nerves, and I saw nothing cute about their antics.

I just couldn't wrap my brain around why seemingly intelligent adults would completely alter their lives just to have kids. I had a great many discussions with different people over the years on this topic. My attitude never wavered, and theirs didn't seem to either. Whoever it was I was talking to invariably told me that it would be different when it was my own kid. I assured them it wouldn't and I would never be finding out.

Right after graduation Marc and I got married, and our lives changed in every way.

I started working like any other business school graduate. I got a full-time job and worked as hard as I knew how to. I was often in my office for sixty hours a week or so. I was constantly fighting for respect, and when I realized it wasn't going to happen, I started to give in. I saw how much more money Marc was making, and it frustrated me. He didn't work harder than I did. He wasn't any smarter than I was. What was the difference?

I worked for a string of bosses who didn't appreciate me or my ability. I personally experienced prejudice because I was Jewish, because I was a woman, and because I was not a part of the family whose business I was working for. I allowed this series of employment experiences to create doubt in myself and lead me to lower expectations in this area of my life. As I had been so driven and focused on career, diminishing these expectations allowed for more time and space in my life for other endeavors and may have contributed to my shift in attitude toward motherhood.

Shortly after we got married, I started riding again and quickly bought the horse of my own I had dreamed of for as long as I could remember. I spent endless hours at the barn from the time I was about twenty-three on. I think that time of my life was similar to the childhood most people experience when they are young.

I hung out with other horse-crazy girls and women, groomed my steed to immaculate perfection, rode around as long as I thought would be acceptable to my mount and trainer, and then started all over again. I would organize my tack, ride extra horses for my friends, even sit and watch other students' riding lessons. I would do anything I could find to do without leaving that wonderful dusty haven with the intoxicatingly pungent scent. I was in the fortunate position of having a husband who made more than enough money to support both of us without question, so I was able to finally live out my childhood dreams.

As the years went on, my sixty hours a week at work became forty, which became thirty-five, and so on. The extra hours I previously spent in the office were now redirected to hours at the barn. By the time of my "light bulb moment," when I was twenty-nine, on the brink of adulthood in my mind, my "career" wasn't much to speak of.

I had a job at an accounting firm. My boss was amazing, and I loved my office and all the people I worked with. But the multiple jobs and frustrations of my past had taken their toll on my confidence and pride. I had interviewed for the position in jeans and cheerfully explained that this was as dressed up as I would be getting. Somehow, my boss was able to recognize my ability and hired me, despite the privileged attitude I displayed.

So, I had a job I loved on Tuesday and Thursday afternoons, where I came after I was done riding my horses. I worked about ten hours a week in my smelly jeans and boots. It was more of a hobby than a career. I could certainly have made it more if I had wanted, but I had kind of fallen into accounting and never particularly enjoyed it. The serious career in the finance industry I pictured in college never really materialized. The few opportunities I had in that area came with major drawbacks that I wasn't willing to accept, so I fell into accounting, which I was very good at but seemed pretty mindless and not what I was meant to be doing.

The barn was "my happy place," where I was calm and found peace, joy, and escape from any conflict or stress in my life. It was so surprising and very distressing that a carefree conversation in this serene haven caused me to question the very direction of my life. This was when I first allowed myself to consider becoming a mother.

Chapter 2

What Now?

———

It is rare to know the exact moment when the path of life veers off in a different direction. When looking back, and only in retrospect, these twists and swerves sometimes show themselves. One hot steamy day in September, 1998, in the expansive arena of my comfortable home horse barn, the path and direction of my life clearly took a sharp turn.

My friend, Jenny, was almost exactly a year older than me, and it was her thirtieth birthday. Jenny was my horse trainer's wife and was one of my favorite people at the barn. She was a tiny girl with straight chestnut hair and a perpetual smile on her face. She was sitting in the middle of a dusty round pen, which is a fenced-off area on one side of the arena. It is set up to keep the horse going in a circle so the trainer can sit in the middle while the horse burns off some excess energy.

A dark brown horse was galloping in a circle, kicking up dust clouds around Jenny, when I arrived at the barn. It was her milestone birthday, and I waded through the deep sand of the arena to get to her before going to find my own mount. I delivered her birthday gift on this warm September day with a sing-song greeting announcing that she was now thirty. She looked at me and said, "You know, you've only got one more year!" I stopped dead in my tracks.

It was a strange turning point in my life. I never realized before what a mental milestone the age of thirty was to me, but somehow when she said that, my life came to a screeching halt.

I'm sure Jenny doesn't even remember the conversation, let alone realize the impact her simple comment had on me. At that exact moment, I realized I was an adult. I mean, she said I was turning thirty in less than a year. That's, like, how old I remember my own mother being. I could clearly recall my mother's thirtieth birthday, and in my perspective, she was very much a grownup with three kids who were not even babies anymore. I looked at my life from entirely new glasses, and I wasn't so happy with what I saw.

This particular September day, I was so busy thinking about the fact that I was no longer a child that I couldn't think of anything else. I rode my beautiful chestnut horse without much attention or joy, which was very unusual, but I just couldn't get that comment out of my mind.

Usually I luxuriated in the feeling of freedom as my mare loped around with my hair flying in the wind. But on this day, I may as well have been sitting in a folding chair. I could only concentrate or focus on what my life had become. I was trying to figure out why I was unhappy and how I might resolve this problem.

The revelation that I would be thirty soon had so knocked me for a loop, I called work and told them I wouldn't be coming in that day.

I thought about it all afternoon but couldn't quite pinpoint what the problem was. I should have been happy, I thought. I was doing exactly what I wanted to be doing, and I was having fun. I had a great husband who made a great living, and we were very comfortable at our lovely house in the expensive suburb where we both grew up.

Because I didn't really have to worry about money too much, I didn't have to work very much myself. I had the freedom to spend my time however I chose. I had the horses in my life I only imagined and longed for in my younger days and a job I genuinely liked and was happy to go to on the afternoons when I went into the office.

I knew how lucky I was to have this life. I was very grateful for my husband, our stability, and the freedom to pursue my dreams. There was absolutely no reason I should feel dissatisfied in any way.

I finally entertained the idea that many of my friends were busy with their children and seemed to really enjoy the connections they were making through school and kids' activities. This must be the answer I was looking for and what was missing from my life. Adults had children, and if I was going to be one, I figured, I should get myself a kid.

I felt confident in this decision when I went home to my husband that night with the news I was dissatisfied with my privileged life. I told him I thought maybe we should have a baby. Why not? Everyone else was doing it, and surely we were just as competent to raise a child as they were.

This declaration was not met with a positive reception. Marc looked at me as if I had just climbed out of the closet and announced it might be a good idea for each of us to cut off an arm. He reminded me of our discussion long ago and that he had changed his plans to exclude children from his future.

Until Marc dated me in college, he had always envisioned himself as any normal student would, with two and a half kids and a dog in his future life. But we made the agreement very early in our relationship that we would move forward together with those kids permanently erased from any future photos of our family that may ever be taken. He changed his perspective on the world and our future back then and had no interest in looking back.

It had been a very long time since our initial discussion of children. We had now been married for eight years, and we had never discussed the subject in our married life. Now Marc told me in no uncertain terms he wasn't going backward. He would not be any part of my plan to have a baby. So rather than argue with him, I reinvestigated my unhappiness and tried to find another way to seek fulfillment.

I thought about my ill-fated career and decided maybe I never should have gone into the area of business and accounting. Again, I traced back my decision to major in finance and examined the other interests of my youth to see what options may have been a better choice for me.

When I was in high school and looking into choosing a field of study, I had been interested in psychology. At that point in my life, I still discussed absolutely everything with my mother. I distinctly remember talking with her about the possibility of pursuing a degree in psychology when I went to college because it was my favorite class in high school. "This would be a very impractical decision for you. To get a job in the social sciences, you need to either get a doctorate or go to medical school," my mother explained.

Since I was a typical teenager in many ways, I was completely fed up with school. I had no interest in committing to anything longer than the four-year degree I was expected to finish. Plus, my mother was quick to remind me, I didn't deal well with the sight of blood, so medical school was completely out of the question.

Well, my second favorite class in high school was a business class. I broached this possibility for a major and got a completely different response. "Oh, that would be a wonderful major for you!" my mother, an accountant, assured me with a huge grin. "You can get a great job right out of college with a degree in business."

According to her, I could quickly and easily earn money, power, and prestige. Well, how could I consider anything else after that review?

After this dissection of my career choices, I realized once again a single discussion had paved my road for many years in this area. I thought about how much I loved my psychology classes, and I looked back at how many of them I had taken as electives in college. I never even realized how strong my attraction to this field had been. Those were my favorite classes all through college, but I had ignored the pull in that direction since my path to complete business school was already set out for me. I had almost enough coursework to have completed a minor in psychology if I had chosen to declare it in college. I decided this was another avenue I may explore to change the pattern of my day-to-day life.

I brought up the idea of going back to school that night at dinner, and while Marc wasn't thrilled at the idea of paying for graduate school, he was certainly excited to find something that would distract me from the idea of having a child.

My course of action was quick and painless for a while. I found a graduate school program I liked and began to pursue a master's degree in counseling psychology. I quit my accounting job and enrolled full time at the Adler School of Professional Psychology.

I really enjoyed being in school again. I got enmeshed in the program and learning how to learn again after years of resting those muscles. I learned to love writing the papers I had dreaded as an undergraduate, partly because I was studying topics that had always interested me, and I was thrilled at the prospect of practicing in a field I actually enjoyed.

Marc joined in my excitement of learning a whole new career. He often helped me proofread my papers and was a sounding board as I delved deeper into the ideas and theories of this new world. He was able to help me assimilate some of the concepts through his scientific mind, and sometimes he would even come to class with me. I felt like this endeavor brought us closer together.

Beyond my love for studying psychology, I was able to use my new knowledge almost constantly in everyday life. I saw my relationships differently and understood more clearly the reasons behind many of my attitudes, opinions, moods, and decisions. As I studied the formation of personality and childhood development, I returned mentally to my interest in having a child of my own.

I had learned my lesson about talking with Marc regarding starting a family the previous summer. I didn't want to hit him over the head again with the idea of having a child. I decided a more indirect approach might work better, so I slowly began to work aspects of parenthood into our discussions. I told him about the classes I was taking and how fascinating it might be to watch a personality take shape. I included him in my preparations for teaching a parenting seminar that was required for one of my credits.

Gradually, I began to mention how having a baby of our own might be something we should try doing at some point in our lives. I guess I wasn't quite as subtle as I had thought I was being, because he made it quite clear: "We are not going to have a baby."

After several months, however, he seemed to come around to my way of thinking. Well, he somewhat came around. He said rather grudgingly, "Okay, *maybe* we can try to get pregnant."

After all, I had assured him we were no longer that young, and it may not be so easy. I was almost thirty, and it would likely take several months, if not longer, to be able to get pregnant. I could not have possibly guessed how wrong this assumption might be.

Chapter 3

We're Having a Baby

___

APRIL 2000

Just two weeks after I harassed Marc into agreeing to try and get pregnant, I thought I should go buy a pregnancy test "just in case." It was the first pregnancy test I had ever bought. Could it be the last I ever bought too? I wouldn't dare to hope it could be so easy.

I had convinced Marc this would be a long process, but I wasn't going to just wait around. I was excited at the prospect we were not using birth control (also for the first time in my life), and it was a possibility that at any time, I could become pregnant. I knew it was just the beginning of our journey, and it might not be easy.

I bought several tests in preparation for the likelihood I would be using them every month for quite some time. I am by nature an impatient person and was not looking forward to months of trying to conceive. However, because it was just the first month, I was trying not to think that far in the future. I just wanted to enjoy this process and couldn't wait to try every part of it.

When I came home from the store, I read through the tiny printed instructions on the box and familiarized myself with the little white plastic stick. I figured I should get used to the idea of taking this kind of test, and maybe I should try one even though it was way too soon for me to be pregnant yet. There couldn't possibly be any harm in doing this.

The box said it should be used first thing in the morning, but I decided to take one of the tests right then anyway, even though it was mid-afternoon. Again, I have never listed patience as one of my great personality strengths. I was really just practicing, after all, so the time of day shouldn't matter.

I brought the box into our newly updated master bathroom and sat on the toilet, rereading the paper insert. The crisp white floor tiles and warm mahogany vanity I chose made me smile and feel more comfortable in the small but cozy room. I was very careful, following the rest of the directions very precisely. I had already broken the first rule on the instructions (that silly morning suggestion), so I was going to learn how to do the rest of the process properly.

I put the stick on the vast white porcelain counter and waited a minute while I washed my hands before even looking at it. This was not a big deal. I couldn't yet be pregnant; I was just learning the process of taking the test. I mentally recorded everything I did because I knew that next month and moving forward, I would be very anxious and would not want to take the time to read instructions. After I checked the little paper booklet again so I would know exactly what I was looking at, I picked up the stick and compared it to the pictures. There were two lines in the window. I looked back and forth between the paper and the stick. Two lines meant I was pregnant!

Wow, I didn't quite know how to handle that idea. I went back into our bright sunny bedroom without noticing the light streaming through the window. Our big four-poster

bed was the same mahogany wood as the bathro
and usually looked warm and inviting. It was co
soft old-fashioned quilt of hand-sewn tiny greer
ple patches of fabric, but today I didn't even notic
matching pillows I had recently purchased or anything else
as I sat on the edge of the bed and stared at the stick.

I honestly had no idea how I felt or what to do. I just didn't
think there was any chance this could happen so quickly.
What did I need to do next? Did I need to go to a doctor? I
didn't even have a doctor.

I had been going to a woman doctor for years, but she
had quit practicing the previous year. I figured I would have
plenty of time to find someone new before I would need
another yearly exam, so I hadn't gotten around to asking anyone for referrals yet. My entire life was going to change, and
I didn't know who to call or how to start getting ready for it!

Okay, first things first. I needed to share this new development with Marc. I knew he wasn't going to jump up, lift
me off my feet, and twirl me around in excitement. He had
only barely agreed to the plan to try and get pregnant two
weeks before. I convinced him (as I truly believed for myself)
that it would likely take several months, at least, before we'd
really be dealing with a pregnancy and a lot longer before
there would be an actual baby. I did think, and hoped, that
there might be some mild pride in his manhood and positive
prospects for the future.

I guess I didn't even consider maybe Marc really had
formed his perspective on the world to include a future
without us ever having children. While we had fought over
whether or not to have children many times in the recent
months, I probably never really believed he had a strong
opinion on the subject. I am so strong in my own beliefs and

opinions that I often steamroll over Marc when it comes to making decisions. Not that I always force him to the choice I prefer, but rather I push him to actually make a decision in one direction or another.

When we decided to buy a car, for example, Marc studied the Sunday paper for weeks. He knew every feature available and how each model compared. We visited a few dealerships and drove a couple of the cars Marc thought looked the best. I went along with his plans for a while. But eventually I took over, and the process changed drastically.

"Let's go look at the new Acura this afternoon!" Marc suggested excitedly on a Saturday morning before I left for the barn. "Sure, as soon as I get home," I replied, without quite the same enthusiasm but hoping it would be the one he liked and we could be done car shopping.

However, it seemed as if each time we drove one car, Marc added at least two more to the list of choices that *might* be the right one for us. "Oh," he said, as we drove down the set route for test drives in the Mazda that felt exactly like the Toyota we had driven just fifteen minutes ago, "if we like this one, there's a Nissan we might like even better, and then we really need to look at the Infinity that's built on the same platform." I nodded silently without admitting that I didn't know what a "platform" was.

While his list of possibilities got quite long, I made it through only a few test drives before my head started to spin. After every vehicle, including the golf cart to take us to the parking lot, felt exactly the same to me, I put my foot down. "Enough! Let me know when you've got it narrowed down to two."

"What? Don't you want to be sure we pick the right one?" he responded incredulously.

"You go drive as many as you want. When you have it narrowed down to two, I will come try them," I told him reasonably.

Of course, this shopping would be no fun by himself, so Marc focused his research to narrow his list as much as he possibly could. He went for a couple more test drives on his own and spent a long time looking at brochures and reviews. Eventually he reported back, "Okay, these three are all *perfect*. Let's go this afternoon so I can show them to you." I joined him, told him the car I liked best, and helped him negotiate a great price (my favorite part).

When it was over, we were happy with the car we bought, and I believed Marc soon forgot about the fifteen models he *thought* he had to personally drive, examine, and evaluate before he could possibly make an informed choice.

This was how most of the big decisions of our life were made. If I didn't force the subject, I don't know if we would ever actually buy a house, car, or pet, or if we would take any vacations, or have any dinner parties. Marc was fine with the small decisions. He could easily choose a movie to rent or decide what to make (or order) for dinner. He was even okay with buying clothes and choosing paint colors. Anything larger than that (especially something really important, like buying a car or—*gasp!*—a television set), required an almost endless amount of research and consideration before Marc could make a final selection.

In fact, if left to his own devices, the purchase may never actually happen because he was simply unable to narrow the possibilities to just one. I have to admit, I have used this to my benefit at times. "You want to wire the whole house for surround sound? Sure, no problem. Just pick out whatever system and speakers you want!" I agreed easily to this request, even though I had absolutely no need for better sound quality. As I expected, it never happened.

So I often fought against his indecision rather than a decision that actually opposed my own. It wasn't that he liked the Toyota better than the Honda. He just wanted to do some more research on the Mazda, Nissan, Suzuki, and Ford before he could even know what he wanted. I made the false assumption that was the case when it came to having a child. I really believed Marc just felt like he needed to do more research and read more parenting books before he'd feel ready to be one himself. I was sure once I put my foot down about actually making the decision and he agreed with my course of action, there would be no looking back. I guess that was why I was not prepared for the reaction I received when I broke the happy news that I was pregnant.

Marc came home from work, plodded upstairs, put down his briefcase, and found me sitting on the bed where I had been all afternoon. "Hey, what's up?" he asked casually.

I tried to be as calm, gentle, and upbeat as I could in my response. "I thought I would just try getting a test to see how it worked so we could be ready to use it next month," I began, but couldn't figure out how to continue, so I just handed him the stick.

"What does this mean?" An edge crept into his voice.

I couldn't answer at first, and I saw his face change as he suddenly shook his head back and forth.

"It means I'm pregnant," I finally pushed the words out quietly.

For a brief moment of silence, he stared in disbelief. After the silence it was like a bomb was dropped. "I knew something like this was going to happen. You told me it would probably take a year or more to get pregnant. I never should have listened to you. After nine years of marriage, you would think I could figure out that I can't trust you. This is not what I want, and I'm not ready!"

After his outburst, Marc stormed out the door and sped down the driveway in his lemon-yellow sports car. Marc loves to drive and doesn't deal well with conflict. He often needs to blow off steam when we get in arguments, so he leaves and goes driving around just for the sake of driving. It upset me mostly because of the lack of control it left me in. Other than that, there really wasn't much to be concerned about. He wouldn't dare put his prized hunk of metal in any danger by drinking before taking it out for a spin.

On this night, though, it felt different than it had before. We hadn't even had an argument. I hadn't said a word beyond the factual report of the lines on a stick. He had sworn at me and run out without listening for any sort of response. While I thought the news would lead to a long discussion and possibly even some mild disagreement, this was a pretty extreme response.

I had visions of sitcoms running through my head. None of the TV husbands ever ran off screaming when their faithful wife of many years announced she was pregnant. This was just weird and not exactly what I thought the monumental beginning of our family would look like.

Marc's reaction and negative attitude actually may have been a good thing for me at the time. Given my general dislike for children and my overwhelming terror at the thought of childbirth, this was probably a good distraction. If he had been more positive about the news, I may have started to question myself and my decision to try this at all. But because I couldn't back down in the face of my husband's temper tantrum, I strengthened my resolve to become a mother.

I couldn't dare show any weakness if this was going to be a disagreement between us.

When Marc returned from his joyride, he was more calm but no more happy. He had accepted an attitude of resignation to his fate. As any good man would, he began to attack the logistics of our future.

"When will we go to the doctor?" he asked pragmatically.

I was forced to admit, "Well, I don't actually *have* an OB/GYN yet."

"How are we going to choose one?" He was starting an actual conversation now. "Is there a calculator to determine the due date? Where will the thing sleep? Are you going to sell your horses? Will you quit your job? Drop out of school?"

Questions I could handle. This was how my husband processed information. I did my best to respond, answering all the questions I could, which seemed to calm him even further, and we began to work together.

We were up late into the morning trying to answer these and countless other questions to the best of our ability with the infinitely limited information we had. I decided that for the time being, Marc's need for details and love of research could be a big help. This was going to be a tough nine months, and we both had no real frame of reference for what any part of our future would look like. I know we didn't have anything to eat that night, but by the morning we had a sketchy blueprint for how to continue.

I had mastered the first two steps of my plan to change my life. Not only had I gotten Marc to agree to the baby idea, but I had an actual human growing inside of me! We could handle it from here. I could plan out the rest of the steps required for "project baby," and we would systematically tackle them one at a time.

Chapter 4

This Is a Doctor?

APRIL 2000

We would need to to find the right doctor to help this baby come into the world. We did organized research, but our well-laid plans somehow led us to the strangest-decorated office I have ever seen. Marc and I laughed so hard I cried, and I suspect that if the pregnancy was any farther along, I may have peed my pants too.

The next step of our plan was to gather what we would need to get through at least the beginning of this pregnancy. We were going to need a doctor—a tour guide to lead us. We agreed that we should begin immediately to do the investigation necessary to find the perfect doctor. I began the search for this doctor and the start of our journey in a very pragmatic, systematic manner, with little emotional involvement. I tried my best to mimic Marc's car-shopping approach of being all-inclusive in my consideration. I would run every possible doctor through my criterion and then take the time to interview all of them who would suit our needs.

I have a tendency to get tunnel vision and focus on one aspect of a problem or decision to come to a resolution. Of course, this selection of an obstetrician was no different.

We had seen a *Dateline* episode about using hypnosis during delivery, and it had convinced us (me) that this would be a requirement to aid in pain relief. The women on the show looked serene and happy, in a semi-trance as she "embraced" each contraction without any indication of discomfort.

"That's for me!" I told Marc.

He rolled his eyes, responding, "I'm sure they got an epidural before they started the hypnosis."

"That's okay with me! I'm going to find one of those hypnosis doctors," I assured him. I didn't care if I had to cook up some meth in the kitchen before heading to the hospital. I would do anything to avoid the childbirth experience my mother had described.

I did gather some recommendations from friends for OBs and midwives they trusted and had a history with. Those were low on the list, though, after the few names that I was able to dig up of practitioners who had experience with the use of hypnotic tools. I used all my resources to find these doctors. I made a special trip to school to meet with the hypnosis professor and get any local names from his address book. I also scoured the internet to find the medical articles on the subject and wrote down the names of any providers in the Chicago area they listed.

I was trying to do the kind of thorough research Marc would recognize and appreciate. I made appointments with every name on my list and planned to visit them all myself but bring Marc only to the three who sounded most promising. After choosing a car, I had learned this narrowing of choices was very helpful. I was hoping that including him in the best visits would make him feel more comfortable with the process and decision.

Excluding him from the ones I thought wouldn't work for us would have the dual benefit of keeping him from getting bored with the process and also avoiding the possibility that he would fall in love with a doctor who wouldn't provide me with the ideal labor experience through hypnosis.

I was going to check off each doctor on the list with a school-like approach. This was a project, and I was going to tackle it with the same drive and determination I used for my master's thesis. Most women might find this task of selecting a doctor very personal and sentimental, seeing it as choosing the guide for bringing their amazing child into the world, but I didn't really consider the life I was creating at all at that point.

I was pretty detached in my thoughts from the idea of actually being a mother to a living, breathing baby. That wouldn't be happening for quite a while. I would first have to tackle all of the choices, tasks, and assignments that would come before I would take on that mother role. In fact, as I looked at my options, my thoughts were 100 percent on myself getting through the pregnancy and childbirth.

The child itself and what would happen after the birth hadn't really entered my thought patterns yet. Marc and I both functioned best in this way. We did well with tasks and projects, especially those that we could break down and complete efficiently.

The first doctor I met with was easy to eliminate as a possibility. Although she was a recommendation of a friend, I couldn't find any reference to hypnosis or alternative pain relief in the online description of her practice. I felt obligated to meet with her because I had asked for the referral, but I didn't even consider bringing Marc. I asked lots of questions, and as I had suspected, she knew basically nothing about even the idea of hypnosis or alternative pain management. Not what I was looking for. I wanted a hypnotist!

I would bring Marc with me on my second meeting, as this doctor was my most promising candidate. I had never even considered using a male OB in the past, but his qualifications transcended his gender. He seemed to be a virtual pioneer in the field of hypnosis use for childbirth. I was able to get an appointment with him quickly, and he even had evening hours so the dads could attend prenatal visits.

Marc and I arrived early and were quite taken aback first by the outside appearance of the office and initial impression when we entered. "Are you sure this is the right place?" Marc asked, so I double-checked the address.

"See?" I responded, showing him the printout with the appointment details, but I understood the question. I couldn't quite believe this was a medical office either, but I wasn't willing to give in to Marc's skepticism just yet.

The street was filled with cafés and trendy shops, all with bright signs announcing their purpose. There were no other simple office spaces or professional type units on the block. The office we were at had the assigned address painted simply on a frosted window with no other identifying information like a name, description, or medical symbol. The door was right on the street just below sidewalk level, so we had to take three steps down to get into the office.

Peering down into the window, we could see a blurry version of the inside through the shading of the frosted glass. It looked to me like a funky resale shop or possibly an odd reseller of foreign tchotchkes, but I marched through the door with confidence.

When we got inside, the waiting room was filled with odd artifacts (maybe fertility gods?) lining shelves on the wall. They were colorful creations of sticks, thread, and beads, most of which resembled primitive dolls or characters, but a few were more similar to dream-catchers or other more decorative pieces.

A plump, friendly, middle-aged receptionist/nurse greeted us and directed us to sit on an old, worn sofa, the type you'd expect to see hungover fraternity brothers lounging on rather than waiting patients. The floor was covered in matted shag carpet, which had obviously been there since it was in style several decades before. In the corner was a sad-looking fireplace that hadn't been cleaned since its last use, but I guessed that the most recent fire had been several winters before.

As we exchanged raised eyebrows and knowing looks, Marc and I swallowed our giggles and tried to look serious. He whispered in my ear, "You think this is our *best* option?" I shrugged in response but was saved from answering when I heard the nurse call out, "Mrs. Asher, we're ready for you."

When we entered the exam room, it got worse instead of better. An exam chair (or was it a table?) sat in one corner of the room. The offending piece of furniture resembled a reclining dentist's chair with stirrups on the far end. The more remarkable feature, however, was the covering for the place I assumed I was supposed to lie down. It was draped with a fake fur that was some sort of cross between a bearskin rug and a slipcover obscuring whatever the original fabric of the chair/table may have once been. Now, that just couldn't be sanitary. Could it?

Also, an old sofa matched the set in the waiting room along with some distressed wood file cabinets and an incongruous simple physician's rolling stool to complete the furnishings. The decor went along with all of the furniture (except for the stool). No white wall or floor tile was to be seen.

More shag in the form of a rug lay on the floor, and each wall had been painted a different autumn-themed color—olive, mustard, brown, and burnt orange. The artwork looked like it belonged in a teepee, and I didn't see a single medical-looking skeleton or diagram of reproductive organs like I was used to seeing in gynecologists' offices in the past. Marc and I both opted to sit uncomfortably on the ugly couch and tried to take in the unusual scene.

When the doctor arrived, he asked the basic questions like when was my due date and who was my previous physician. We gave him all of our vital information and told him we were expecting our first child in about eight months. This relatively normal exchange and gathering of information convinced us that it might be okay. We both took a deep breath and felt ourselves starting to believe that this man may have actually attended medical school. After we answered all of the "typical" medical questions, we explained that we had found him on the internet and were very interested in the use of hypnosis during labor.

Just when Marc and I began to feel like maybe we weren't in the twilight zone, the conversation took a definite shift downhill. "We're very interested in learning more about how hypnosis can reduce the pain levels during labor and delivery," I continued the discussion.

The doctor, whose skin looked like it had seen too much sun in his childhood and whose long hair and outfit suggested that he might be heading to Woodstock after our appointment, replied with a calm voice, "Why would you think there would be pain?"

I did a double-take. No pain? Did he think we were here just to pee on a stick?

"Why are you worried about this?" he continued. "Hypnosis can help you to relax so you can both enjoy the experience."

I didn't quite know how to respond to that. I remembered my mother's description of childbirth—blood, guts, stitches, ripping, and unimaginable pain. What was I missing here? But I tried to be professional. "I have a very low pain tolerance and would probably want lots of medication as well." I went on, somewhat ignoring his previous comment.

He interrupted me, "There you go, using that word again. I just don't understand why you think there will be *pain* in childbirth." Those were his exact words. I couldn't make this up. I will never forget this extraordinary response to the very vulnerable admission of my fears.

Now, let me stop here to say I had always felt I wouldn't want to see a male OB/GYN because they had never experienced what I would be going through. I felt even stronger at this point I should have stuck to that rule. I realized I had never been through childbirth either as of yet, and I hadn't even been present at a live birth of any kind. Yet somehow I seemed to have a much more clear view of what to expect than this man who happened to have a medical degree and had observed at least hundreds of deliveries with his own eyes.

I also felt for the first time in a while, Marc and I were thinking along the same lines. I was sure he couldn't wait to get out of there either. I could see him taking copious mental notes about every aspect of the office and the doctor so we could laugh about this for a long time to come. I felt the visit actually brought us closer together, although it got us no closer at all to finding an appropriate agent to assist us through our impending ordeal of the next several months.

So, the conversation continued along these lines for almost an hour. Our guide (he didn't like to call himself "doctor") told us how bringing a child into the world was the most amazing experience a couple would ever have. He stressed the equal (excuse me?) roles both parents played in the process, claiming somehow Marc holding my hand and speaking words of comfort was just as difficult (well, he said exciting and wonderful) as me pushing a watermelon-sized human out of an opening that I felt strongly should not accommodate anything larger than a zucchini.

He also rambled on about how beautiful the delivery would be. He said while some women experience mild discomfort during the miracle of birth, it was just a wonderful feature to get her attention and make her appreciate the adventure she should be cherishing and enjoying.

After talking to us for so many minutes and seeing the joint expression of disgust and surprise on both of our faces, this man couldn't be more certain we should *not* become parents. We were not at all appreciative of the amazing journey upon which we were just embarking and couldn't possibly do a responsible job of savoring every aspect from that moment through the next eighteen years or so.

He insisted upon giving me a quick pregnancy test, and I would have bet money he was hoping for a negative result. The nurse came into the room and said, specifically, "You got the result you wanted. You are definitely pregnant." She then asked when we would like to schedule our next appointment. We assured her as we were running out the door that we would call her after we checked our calendars.

Well, we laughed all the way home. We were smiling and on the same page for the moment. This support and camaraderie between the two of us would be very important in the very near future.

Chapter 5

This Can't Be Good

———

For three days after our appointment at the doctor's office with the extensive shag carpet and carved fertility gods, Marc and I would randomly start laughing for no reason. Marc shook his head, muttering, "We have *equal* roles in childbirth?" out of the blue during dinner. "Why would I think there would be pain during labor and delivery?" I responded as we both rolled our eyes.

The laughter from our joint doctor appointment had barely died down when our journey took another sharp turn, and we weren't laughing as the walls of the tenuous peace we had created came crashing down.

We were sure any future doctor interviews would be more productive, if not more memorable. Our next appointment was scheduled for about a week later, and we joked that if it wasn't a bit more reasonable, our search might take longer than we expected.

Unfortunately, our quest for the perfect doctor was cut short. Just three quick days after our only joint interview, I needed a medical professional immediately. My carefully crafted calendar of doctor interviews, appointments, and continued research got thrown out the window. I would not have the luxury of actually making an informed decision about who our doctor would be. I would be forced to make a sudden split-second choice and rely on my gut.

While I had finished the prescribed coursework for my master's degree, I was also required to do a year of practical internship. I was working as a therapist on the inpatient mental health floor of a hospital to fulfill this requirement.

On a Friday just before lunch, I was working with a patient in a tiny, windowless room. We sat on mismatched rolling chairs with a small desk between us and were talking about triggers and how to deal with events that led to negative thinking. I had just gotten a pad of paper and had asked the middle-aged man to brainstorm ideas of calming activities. I added to his list of strategies for managing anxiety but had only gotten a couple of ideas written down. I suddenly felt a mild stabbing pain in my abdomen. I quickly finished the session, telling the patient to finish brainstorming the list as "homework" and we could discuss it on Monday.

I rushed down the hall, practically running past doctors and nurses. I fumbled with my keys trying to open the door to my sun-filled cozy office, where I had a private bathroom. I thought I just may have diarrhea or something but saw blood as soon as I sat down on the toilet.

What does this mean? I thought as I sat there in pain. *Is something wrong? Am I going to need some sort of procedure or medication?* So many possibilities ran through my head uncontrollably. I dragged the corded industrial telephone across the small office and literally made calls from the attached bathroom while I continued to bleed into the toilet.

I had a friend who had recommended a nurse practitioner/midwife very highly. My friend, Colleen, had assured me this woman was very gentle and kind and would hold my hand through everything. I needed my hand held right now. She was on my list to interview but didn't have an appointment available for almost six weeks. So, I had never met this woman and didn't even have an initial interview/appointment scheduled for several more weeks.

I called anyway, and the panic must have been evident in my tone as I spoke to the voice on the phone. "I'm not actually a patient yet. I have an appointment in May. But I'm pregnant and I'm *bleeding*! I don't know what this means, but I'm sure it can't be good. I don't know who else to call...." the words came spilling out. I was trying to explain calmly, but I knew I didn't sound calm. The receptionist, who sounded like a gentle grandma, could tell that it was an emergency and put me right through to the midwife.

I must have sounded quite pathetic because I was crying as I explained that this woman had no idea who I was. I told her I had my first appointment scheduled with her the following month, but I couldn't wait that long. "I know I'm pregnant. I took a test and they even took one when we went to interview another doctor, and both were positive. But for some reason I am bleeding. I don't know what to do! Do I need to take something?"

Just as Colleen had described, she was very serene and comforting. "Spotting at this point isn't always an indication of a problem. It may mean nothing, but we should definitely check just to be sure. I'll send an order over right now to have some levels tested in your blood."

I explained where I was and that I could have blood drawn downstairs (one of the benefits of working in a hospital).

She assured me she would make time to see me on Monday, and she also promised to call as soon as she received the test results.

I felt only a little better after talking to her, but she comforted me enough that I could breathe now. I took a deep breath and headed downstairs to have my blood drawn. The blood draw was an event itself, as the nurse was not the best and had to try both arms before actually extracting a small amount of blood from the vein on the back of my hand.

"This will have to do!" She thought it should be enough, even though they usually take several times the amount she was able to eek out of my sad, tiny veins. When I got back to my office, I was frustrated, scared, and completely unsure how to feel.

I dragged the clunky phone back from the bathroom and called Marc as I sat at my simple wood desk. "I started having some cramping and bleeding," I tried my best to explain clearly to Marc without crying.

"Let's not worry about this until we know there's really a problem." He did his best to comfort and assure me it might be nothing. He was able to convince me I should not be worried yet since we really didn't even know if anything was wrong until after the test results came back. There was my logical scientist husband again. I hung up with him, sighed deeply, and tried to quiet the voice screaming in my head, telling me to panic.

Luckily, I had an old but clean and comfortable sofa in my office, because all of the anxiety and sheer panic I was feeling had completely exhausted me. I asked another intern to meet with my patients and cover my groups for the rest of the afternoon, and I actually laid down on the sofa with the sun shining in my eyes from the window just above it and fell asleep for over an hour. When I woke up, I still didn't feel right but thought I could manage driving home.

At this point, I felt as if I couldn't even see the path in front of me. I had no idea what this bleeding might mean or what I may possibly learn on Monday. The signs were just not clear to me. I thought we had a pretty open route in front of us, but I was starting to feel like we had hit a detour of some sort.

Chapter 6

More Than One

Suddenly this process became more personal. We had been acting as if this was just a project, finding the right doctor and planning for how to proceed. Now it seemed like there was a lot at stake here. For the first time I realized that even though I had gotten pregnant, it wasn't a 100 percent sure thing I would tough it out for nine months and a baby would appear. There was some risk here, and I was starting to think the end result was something that needed to be protected. I would need to do my best to distance myself from these thoughts if I was going to make it through even the next several hours.

When the midwife finally called the next day, I had been eating my nails and cuticles until they bled. This had never even been a habit before, but desperate times called for desperate measures. She said my progesterone levels were on the low end of normal, but she would check them again on Monday to be sure. Other than that, the tests looked pretty good and I should try to relax for the next day and a half.

I did feel better after talking with her and managed to survive until my appointment two days later. On Monday I met the nurse who was also the lovely older woman answering the phone three days earlier and graciously putting me through to the midwife. I was correct that she reminded me of my grandma and was just as kind. She made me feel so comfortable while she gathered my information and vitals before she led me to the simple cramped examining room.

The midwife squeezed into the tiny, bare room and started by lecturing me on her whole pregnancy rules and suggestions. Normally I would have complained and argued, but after the scare I had, I was willing to agree to drinking eighty-four glasses of water each day if that was what I was supposed to do.

After I got undressed, the midwife did an exam and said my uterus felt large for my estimated due date. Her exact comment was, "I wonder if there may be more than one."

This didn't sink in at all, and I laughed as I replied, "More than one what, uterus?" Then it hit me what she was saying. "Baby?" No, that simply wasn't possible. I had barely gotten Marc to agree to one baby. I would have to leave the extra one at the hospital if there were two. In fact, Marc was a twin and never enjoyed having a clone in his life. This would not be a welcome piece of news.

The midwife, who clearly didn't know me, said I could get an ultrasound then or wait to be surprised. I do not like surprises! I called the number she gave me for an ultrasound technician from my cell phone while I was walking out the door of her office. I couldn't wait until I got to the car. I needed to drive straight there and get an answer *now*.

For some reason, the ultrasound technician did not seem to think this situation was urgent. I was nothing short of flabbergasted by her attitude. How could this not be an emergency? The alien inside me might be *two* aliens! What could possibly be more of an emergency? I wasn't able to keep my voice steady as I explained that I could not possibly wait until the following morning. I needed to get an appointment today! I was again on the brink of crying, which now seemed to be turning into a habit.

I was no longer worried about the progesterone levels, which I was told would just need to be monitored. I needed to be sure that I wasn't going to have to find a home for my poor baby's surprise sibling who may or may not exist. She eventually agreed that if I came right away she would squeeze me in.

I made panicked calls to both my husband and sister-in-law on my way to the ultrasound appointment.

I called Marc first and I could tell he was not so thrilled. He was a bit cold and curt as he murmured, "I only agreed to having one baby. And being a twin is not all it is cracked up to be." He also started down the road of "what ifs," which made me even more nervous. "Where would both babies sleep?" "How could we take care of two at once?" "Can we afford to buy two of everything?" He already had my stomach churning, but when I pressed him, he backed off. "Just call me after the ultrasound, and we can talk about this when we know for sure."

His lack of enthusiasm mirrored my own, although I certainly didn't let this information slip while I was talking to him! I had to be the gung-ho enthusiastic mommy-to-be if I was going to convince him (and myself) I was thrilled about all of this and was not at all questioning my decision to get pregnant.

Joan, my sister-in-law and the wife of Marc's twin, was more supportive. Joan has been a part of my life since we were both dating "the boys" in college. Just after I started dating Marc, I transferred to Indiana University. Shortly after I arrived, Joan found me. Through Marc's mom she had learned I would be living in the very same dorm where she lived! She came over, introduced herself, and learned that I had a car.

I saw a twinkle in her eye when she asked, "Are you planning to go see Marc anytime soon? I'd be happy to go with you." Both Marc and Rob, his twin, attended the University of Illinois, about a two-and-a-half-hour drive from us. Joan had been dating Rob for years, and because she didn't have a car herself, visits to U of I were uncommon luxuries. Since my relationship with Marc was new and exciting, I was game to make the drive often!

Soon it became our regular weekend plan to make the trek out Friday night and spend two wonderful days with our "boys." We spent a lot of hours in the car together, and we soon became close friends. Eventually we were bridesmaids in each other's weddings.

Joan has stayed a wonderful friend and my closest confidant in Marc's family. She is even shorter than me, with smooth white skin and a crown of auburn curls. She is also an incredibly upbeat person with unmatched patience and tolerance that I have often admired.

Joan reassured me, "You will be fine with whatever you get. So many people can't get pregnant at all or have to go through major drugs and procedures to have a baby." She started telling me all kinds of stories about many of her friends who had resorted to multiple rounds of IVF after years of trying to conceive; they spent so much money, and one friend was even thrilled to end up with triplets.

She tried to persuade me I should be grateful and appreciate how I had been blessed. She didn't convince me, but I had to admit to feeling better. More than that, she kept me distracted and entertained during my drive so I didn't freak out on the highway.

The ultrasound office was a small, unremarkable storefront in a strip mall. I jumped out of the car and entered a tiny waiting area, where I was called in immediately from a disembodied voice behind an open door. I went through the doorway toward the voice and found myself in the actual room where the ultrasound machine itself lived. The exam room was very simple, dark, and depressing.

I did not enjoy my first introduction to an internal ultrasound, but I was willing to go through just about anything to find out how many babies were inside me. The ultrasound technician was able to tell me there was only one egg sac, but it was so early, the embryos were not yet clearly visible. This meant while identical twins were not able to be ruled out, they were much more unlikely than fraternal twins, which were not possible with a single sac. She said a follow-up visit in a couple of weeks could be justified to rule out twins completely, especially given my questionable progesterone levels.

My fears were calmed enough that I was able to take a deep breath and return to my previous business-like demeanor. I started asking lots more questions now that I didn't need to spend all my effort trying not to cry. I was reasonably satisfied only one baby was in there, and no one seemed to be fussing about the progesterone levels or spotting from the previous week, which had since ceased.

I was able to begin believing this had all just been a big inconvenience and was going to turn out as I'd planned after all. I'd just need to monitor the progesterone and return for another ultrasound, which should confirm the presence of a single baby and also further ease my fears by allowing me to see the fetus again.

Those progesterone levels were definitely going to be cumbersome to me, but at this point I had returned to my professional role of mommy-to-be and had relinquished the emotional basket case I had become over the weekend, at least temporarily.

The midwife wanted my blood taken every three days. Before the past month, I hadn't had a needle stuck in my body for a great many years. I didn't do well with needles of any kind, especially with having blood taken. As I mentioned, the first time they took blood had not gone well at all. Unfortunately, this turned into a pattern each time I went to the hospital to become a human pincushion.

I had a lot of anxiety about what my levels would show each time, so I was on constant pins and needles, so to speak.

Things went okay for a short while, but before it was even time for the next ultrasound, the progesterone levels dropped even more. My midwife—who I now had hired, cancelling any appointments I had made with other doctors… so much for that hypnosis idea—said I should use a progesterone supplement to raise the levels. This could only be done through a vaginal suppository twice a day, which didn't sound like a lot of fun, but I had become a bit more compliant than normal. I wasn't going to let any inconvenience interfere with my goal. I was trying to be a team player here, so if the doctor said to use a device that looked like a tampon for inserting goo, I would take one for the team.

I don't really think I understood clearly that I was protecting the pregnancy and I could miscarry if the levels remained low. My head just didn't go in that direction. I had no experience with being pregnant, after all.

My whole life I had been taught if you ever dared to have sex without birth control, you would get pregnant and have a baby. That's pretty much what had happened too—at least so far—so it didn't occur to me that having a baby wouldn't follow automatically. In fact, I now know that at least 10 percent of early pregnancies end in reported miscarriage, and the true number is likely much higher. Who knew? Why didn't anyone ever tell me this? I don't know what I thought would happen if I didn't follow instructions for getting the hormone levels up. I guess I just didn't let my thoughts drift that far into the future.

After I started the supplement, my levels did go up. I stopped worrying as much, even though my midwife was still having my blood tested several times a week. I don't really know why I wasn't more concerned about this at the time. Joan, who had two small kids, did tell me she only had one blood test in each of her two pregnancies, so it wasn't like I didn't know this was not the normal protocol. I guess I figured they were overly cautious about everything, and different doctors may have different practices for tests.

After about three weeks, I went back for another ultrasound. The technician looked at the screen and did some measurements. It seemed very quick to me, and of course I asked lots of questions. The technician didn't want to show me much but said I should call my doctor.

I pressed her on it, and she finally admitted the egg sac hadn't grown enough in the three weeks. "That's no big deal," I quipped. "It must just be a small baby." She tried to gently explain to me that the growth in the first trimester is very predictable, and mine didn't appear to be growing any more.

I called my midwife to talk about what this meant. "Most likely the fetus is no longer growing," she explained.

"I'm sure the baby is just small and needs more time to grow," I assured her.

"That's not how it works. The measurements from today show the fetus is no longer viable. You don't need to continue with the prenatal vitamins and the progesterone supplement," she continued.

I refused to believe her. "Really," I interrupted her, "it could just be a small baby. We need to keep trying to help it." I couldn't possibly accept this diagnosis.

"Well, it won't hurt you to continue for one more week, and then we can do another ultrasound just to confirm," she finally relented. She was just humoring me, but I didn't recognize that at the time.

After another week of complete denial on my part, I was able to go have another ultrasound. This time she told me to just go to her office for the ultrasound. This should have been an indication to me that she was just placating me, but again I was oblivious.

"There isn't any growth here," she reported quietly. "The multiplication of cells in the first trimester is extremely predictable in a healthy pregnancy. That is not what we are seeing here." She was very gentle and kind, and it was obvious from her demeanor that she was only completing this exercise to help me accept what was going on.

I finally said I understood, although I didn't accept it in my heart. She said I could schedule a D&C, where they would scrape out my uterus, or I could just wait to miscarry. Since I was still convinced there was some hope the baby would start growing again, the choice was easy. I would wait and see what happened. Somehow I believed I could *will* the baby to grow. "I'll show everyone. My baby is just tiny and needs a little extra time to get bigger."

I was hysterical every night, and my dreams were all haunted by visions of a tiny, misshapen baby, but during the day I went on like nothing had happened. This could not have been a healthy way to handle things emotionally. After the two weeks elapsed, the midwife called me to see how I was doing. She had asked me to call her when I started bleeding, but she hadn't heard from me.

When I confirmed I had not seen any blood, she finally took a slightly more controlling tone as she explained to me, "There is no way the fetus is still alive or growing at this point."

When I continued to question her, she said forcefully, "Jennifer, do you really want to continue walking around carrying dead tissue inside of you?" She was no longer asking. "I am scheduling you for a D&C. My nurse will call you back to let you know when the procedure will be."

I wasn't happy about it but grudgingly agreed. Unfortunately, it was now almost the beginning of July, so the holiday was causing all kinds of problems for the operating room schedule. I would need to wait another week or so before the procedure would take place. I also made the midwife agree to do one final ultrasound the day beforehand, just to make sure there wasn't any further growth. This should have shown her and anyone else the level of denial that I was in. I just couldn't believe I wasn't going to have this baby!

Of course, the final ultrasound showed what everyone besides me already knew. There was no growth over the three weeks since the last one. My midwife had returned to her kind and gentle tone, "You just need to accept this and move on. We will proceed with the D&C tomorrow. Do you have any questions about what will take place?"

I then—finally—became extremely anxious about the impending procedure. As I said, I don't deal well with needles, and I really was not looking forward to having an operation. I asked every friend I could think of what would happen and got lots of very different answers.

I was surprised at how many of my friends had already had this procedure at some point in their life. About half of the friends I talked to were able to tell me about their own experience. Some women said it really wasn't a big deal, and I didn't need to worry. Most, however, said it was pretty uncomfortable and they had substantial bleeding and cramping afterward.

I got to the hospital about eight o'clock in the morning. It was a typical hospital, very cold and sterile. I filled out all kinds of forms, and we waited around for a while—first in the general waiting room, which was a large room like you'd find at any doctor's office, and then in the outpatient surgery waiting room, which was a smaller room and less decorated with only simple uncomfortable chairs to sit on, and finally in a "temporary" hospital room, which wasn't really a room at all but more like an "area" separated from the rest of the room on three sides by hanging light blue curtains. We just kept waiting.

We didn't have much to talk about, and pretty much everything Marc said just irritated me. He was trying to keep up a happy chatter. "Wasn't that nurse nice? Look at that interesting lighting fixture. I didn't realize you could see the lake from here. The tree right outside the window is so pretty and blooming. Do you know if those are cherry blossoms?" He kept on asking questions despite the fact that I responded only with grunts or shrugs. I felt badly about being annoyed, but I couldn't believe I wasn't going to be having this baby. Nothing else at all seemed important enough to waste any breath on. Finally I was asked to change into a hospital gown and sign a consent form.

After signing the form, I felt a warm liquid go through my IV, and I closed my eyes.

The next thing I knew I was back in my temporary hospital room with Marc at my side, and I didn't feel any different. I needed to eat something and go to the bathroom before they would let me go home, so I did my best to comply.

As I was eating my required bagel and cream cheese, an older woman who looked like she had just stepped out of 1960 came into my room. She had long gray hair that fell easily down to the small of her back and was wearing bell-bottom pants with her striped blouse. She explained she was a social worker, and she was there to help me cope with my grief. I told her I really wasn't interested, but she wouldn't leave. I explained I was in graduate school for psychology and also was in therapy once a week, but it didn't seem to register with her.

She kept going on about the support groups and hotline they have set up to talk about my loss. *Now come on, is this really necessary?* I definitely did not have the energy or attention to even hear what she was saying. This woman wouldn't leave my room until the doctor finally arrived, and I told her I had confidential questions to discuss.

I felt fine and barely had any bleeding from the surgery. It was like nothing had happened at all, like the baby never even existed.

I was on autopilot that entire summer. I continued my internship and worked with many patients at the hospital. I can't recall much of anything about the individuals or cases, but I hope my schooling had been thorough enough that I took good care of them.

I also returned to my horses and showing them, but my heart wasn't in it the way it was before. The ribbons, trophies, and even the joy and freedom of flying across the field on my horse didn't fulfill me anymore. I now knew my purpose in life was to become a mother.

I was told I'd have to wait a cycle or two before trying to get pregnant again. I tried to be patient waiting for my period to return and tracking the time until it would be safe to get back on our quest to parenthood. I went through the motions of my life without much thought or intention, focused on a single goal to the exclusion of all others. I *would* get pregnant again, as soon as possible.

Chapter 7

One More Try

___

AUGUST–NOVEMBER 2000

My mission had hit a small bump in the road, but I was not going to be derailed! I was on a journey to become a mother, here. No little miscarriage would get in my way. I could not allow Marc to drag me off my path either. Come on, team baby. I would be pregnant again before Marc or I could question or second-guess ourselves.

Once I finally got another period, I casually mentioned to Marc that we could try to get pregnant again. "Really?" he questioned. "How well did that work for us the first time? Did you want to go through all of that *again*?" He tried to convince me maybe we should just forget about it. "You were not very fun to live with last spring," he continued.

Obviously he wasn't understanding this was the only thing I had thought about for the past several months. "It will be different this time," I tried to assure him. "The last time was just a fluke. I know next time will be a lot easier."

We eventually compromised and agreed we would try *only* one more time. I promised if the pregnancy wasn't successful, I would give up on trying to carry a baby. Although

I agreed to this, I was sure it wouldn't happen. There was no way I would allow a second miscarriage.

I wanted the new pregnancy to be completely different from the first time, so I tried taking a different approach to pretty much everything.

I found a new midwife before I was even pregnant. I had really liked the personal attention I received from my first midwife, even though it didn't end well. As nice as she was, I wanted to make a fresh start. I also decided I wanted to go to a completely different hospital. Although it was a bit farther away from our home, I didn't think it would make much difference, and I wanted nothing to be the same as the last time.

I found a wonderful midwife named Molly, who had an office near my house as well as one downtown near the hospital. It was a perfect situation. Molly was so easy to work with. She had a fresh girl-next-door look with wavy blonde hair and a gentle smile that made her very easy to relate to and confide in. She was young, pretty, and extremely patient—always allowing as much time as I needed to chat and answer every possible question. I was happy to have her on my team.

I got pregnant easily again, and things seemed to be going well. As soon as I saw those two lines on the little plastic stick in early October, Molly wanted to test my blood regularly due to my previous experience. My progesterone levels were quite high this time, and I had no problems at all. She continued to monitor every three days, just to make sure, even though she assured me it would be very unlikely for me to miscarry again. I was absolutely positive everything was going to continue to be night and day different from the first pregnancy disaster.

The blood draws continued to be difficult, and I dreaded going twice a week. It was worth it, though, because the reports showed my hormone levels to be high and good. I felt great, wasn't sick at all, and finally started to relax. I had no spotting, no cramping, no strange stabbing pains. I was sure this time was totally different.

One Saturday morning in November, though, I got a call from Molly. She sounded close to tears as she told me my levels had completely dropped on my last test. I refused to believe her. I'd had no signs this time at all. I didn't feel any different than I had for the previous several weeks while the levels were great, so how could they have changed suddenly?

I asked if I could go on the progesterone supplement, but she said it was too late. There was nothing more I could do but wait to miscarry. I had heard this before. I was not looking forward to the next few weeks of waiting. I tried to convince myself it must be a mistake or mix-up at the lab, and Molly agreed to have the levels re-tested on Monday.

"Just take it easy this weekend," she advised me. "Try to relax and get some rest. I'm so sorry this happened to you again." She seemed to be taking this much harder than I was. Of course, there was no reason for me to take things easy, or to be upset, because this was some kind of mistake and would all be cleared up on Monday. I would show her, and everything would be fine again.

I told Marc about my call from Molly before we went to the mall that day, but I assured him I felt fine and it was all a big mistake. We followed the path around the dimly lit enclosed mall, dodging oblivious teenagers and families pushing strollers as we ducked into a few random crowded shops.

I felt like a zombie trolling the mall, not even seeing the crowds of people around me or any of the cute new cruise-wear being shown in the shop windows. Nothing felt real, and I couldn't focus on the running commentary coming from my husband. I was doing my best to play the role of happy wife, but I think I was failing pretty miserably.

I was trying my best to act normal and show some interest in the new socks and dessert plates we had purchased. "Let's stop and get a smoothie for lunch," I suggested, so we headed to the noisy open food court. Just as Marc was ordering the "Mango-a-go-go," I felt some cramping in my abdomen.

I rushed to the large, echoing bathroom near the food court. As soon as I sat down, blood and chunks of tissue fell into the toilet. I was embarrassed and upset and didn't know what to do. Someone had told me to save the tissue because if it was the actual baby, they could do testing on it. I was crying hysterically but leaned over the cold porcelain toilet and scooped what I could into toilet paper, wrapped it into a huge bundle of paper, and stuck it in my purse. This baby thing had gotten *way* messier than I expected, and I wasn't even close to the delivery part yet.

I washed my hands very thoroughly after that (yuck!) with tears streaming down my cheeks and tried to calm down. A woman came into the bathroom and asked if I was okay. I snapped at her quite rudely, and she quickly rushed right back out the door. I finally collected myself, walked out of the bathroom, and simply told Marc that I needed to go home.

For once, he didn't ask any questions. He could tell from my pale and vacant face I didn't want to talk about anything. He found a chair for me to wait on and sprinted across the huge mall to get the car and bring it around for me in record time. We sat in silence on the way home, and I was grateful he didn't press me for any details. If he had tried to talk to me, I would have either bitten off his head or burst into hysterical tears. Probably both.

"It's over," I whispered simply to Marc before heading to bed. It was only two o'clock, but I was so upset and drained that I slept through the afternoon until past midnight.

When I finally woke up, I remembered what had happened. I didn't wake Marc or get anything to eat. I went straight to our home office across the hall from the bedroom and turned on the computer. I had been told, twice now, that I was not meant to carry a child, and I wouldn't question it again. I had passed the fork in the road and was all ready to charge down a new path full steam ahead.

Chapter 8

Let's Adopt

NOVEMBER 2000

According to Adoption Network's "US Adoption Statistics," about 2 percent of children in the United States were adopted (Adoption Network, 2021). Our child would be all the more special to be chosen by us rather than grown inside me.

I didn't realize the huge step I was taking that night. I didn't think about my options or weigh them carefully. I did not talk to fertility specialists, have testing done on Marc's body or mine, or attempt any alternative methods of conceiving a child. I didn't have months of discussion with Marc about whether or not we could love a child that was not biologically ours.

I had no interest in soul-searching. Clearly I was not meant to have a baby of my own, and that was quite simply the end of that. Marc had agreed after the first miscarriage that we could adopt a child if a second pregnancy didn't work, and I wasn't going to loose any time arguing about whether or not to move forward. I had wasted more than six months since Marc and I agreed to have a baby, and I wasn't going to waste another minute!

I had a home office set up with two desks on opposing walls and matching office chairs with file cabinets at each. Marc and I shared this space but rarely worked in here together at the same time. Bookshelves lined the walls, and the room was sunny and bright with white paint and lots of windows. The office had always been an easy place for me to sit quietly and get my schoolwork done. There was no sunlight at midnight, but it was still a serene room with few distractions keeping me from my task at hand.

I sat down at my desk and started to search the internet for sites about adoption. I had an idea in my head about not wanting to adopt within the United States, and I had a couple of reasons behind this idea. First, I get very easily emotionally involved with people and couldn't stand the thought of a birth mom changing her mind after the baby was born. I also didn't like the idea that I would have to compete with other families for a birth mom to choose us.

Also according to Adoption Network's "US Adoption Statistics," it is estimated that between one and two million families in the US are waiting to adopt, and only about 135,000 domestic adoptions happen each year (Adoption Network, 2021). I didn't like those odds, and I also felt compelled to actually "save" a child that might not otherwise get adopted. I had made the decision it would be best for our family to grow through international adoption before I even turned on the computer.

I don't know if I consciously thought very hard about adopting before that day, because I hadn't allowed myself to believe I wouldn't be delivering my own child. I don't think I had much discussion with Marc about adopting a child, or even internal discussions with myself. I must have subconsciously considered it, though, because I already seemed to have a good idea about where and how I wanted things to go.

I was up most of the night learning what I could from the internet about international adoption. I wrote down lists of phone numbers that it frustrated me I would have to wait to call. *Why doesn't everyone work on the weekends?* I continued this research all the next day and late into the night. Marc peeked in on me several times but just shook his head and ducked back out of the room. He knew I was upset and that it would be dangerous to get in my way. He could also see the writing on the wall—there would be a baby in our house before too long, regardless of how my body chose to act.

By Monday morning I had a whole sheet of paper filled with phone numbers to call and questions to ask. I thought from my research that I wanted to adopt from China, and I wanted to find the fastest way to do it. I called in sick to work and school (blaming my miscarriage), and plowed ahead like a bulldozer on a mission.

In one day, I spoke with approximately eight different agencies and called families each agency gave me as references. I wanted to go to China because there were so many baby girls there whose families were unable to keep them, and in general the babies from China were very healthy. However, the agencies I spoke with quoted a very long waiting time to get a baby. Being the hardheaded person I was, I was sure there must be a way around this. No communist government could get in my way! Some agency must have a "back door" shortcut to make a Chinese adoption proceed more quickly, and I was going to find it.

My internet crash course had also taught me a lot about the process of adoption in general. I learned I would need to have a home study done right away before I could submit a dossier. (See, I was even learning the language!)

The home study is a report put together usually by a social worker. The social worker would meet with the family several times, gathering tons of information about both parents and extended family. She would also tour the home and see where the baby would live as well as checking references given by the family and gathering various reports such as notes from our doctors, claiming we were healthy enough to raise a child. After all of that, she would put together a report, called a "home study," saying that the family met all the state's requirements to adopt a child.

The dossier is more of a collection of documents required by the country where the child is born. This often includes original birth certificates for the parents, marriage license, social security cards, background checks, letters of recommendation, documents showing financial standing, etc., and includes the home study itself.

Several country-specific documents may also be in the country's native language, which need to be completed by the parents, agency, or some other person and included in the dossier. Within all of this paperwork, some documents need to be notarized, some need state seals, and eventually the whole thing needs to be sent to the embassy of the child's country to be officially translated into their home language.

I called and interviewed several local agencies who were licensed to do home studies in our area. I chose one—of course the one who said they could do it the fastest—and made our first appointment.

By the time Marc got home from work Monday night, I had the calendar filled with workshops to attend, visits to agencies planned, and an evening in about a week when the home study worker would be coming by for the first time. Marc was not as impressed as I wanted him to be.

"We need to do some research on this," he said.

"Already done," I replied.

"We need to choose a country," he continued.

"China," I told him.

"Have you thought about what I want?" he asked. I explained to him that I knew what he wanted. Through our previous, though limited, conversations I knew his concerns and preferences. Obviously it was important to both of us to have a healthy child, and I also knew it was important to him for any travel required to be minimally intrusive to his work schedule. I took all of this into account, did the research, and knew China was the direction we wanted to head in.

"I have three agencies I want to talk to some more, and I'm happy to include any questions you have too," I told him before he could object further.

He continued to fire questions at me, which I answered based upon the research I had already done and what the agencies told me. Finally he quieted, realizing I would have an answer for every concern he had. We had been married long enough—about ten years—and Marc knew there was no getting me off track once I had set my sights on a destination.

In my head I was still beating myself up a bit. I clearly did not do enough to make the pregnancy path work for us. I hadn't been prepared enough, and I must have made mistakes along the way that interfered with the pregnancies. I was sure of it. I must have missed something that the doctors didn't tell me about, but I was *not* going to make the same mistake in the adoption process.

I would cross every t and dot every i. I was going to have a baby, and no detail would be overlooked. I may not have complete control over my body, but paperwork was something I could manage. I had timelines, spreadsheets, lists, and printouts. I could do this, and there would be no stopping me.

Marc wasn't very happy that things seemed to be moving so quickly, but he agreed to accompany me to the various appointments and workshops I had arranged and already added to the calendar on the refrigerator. We could finally discuss the fun things, like what our child would be like and what an adventure it would be to travel to a foreign country and learn more about their way of life.

The mood seemed to lighten after Marc accepted his fate. We talked about how much we liked Asian culture and how much fun it would be to go to China with a group of other families who were all adopting children as well. We fantasized about what it would be like to have a little Chinese daughter and how much we would teach her about everything. We planned for how the Chinese New Year was going to become an important holiday for us. We talked about how we could arrange our house to make room for the baby and even how we would decorate her room.

Okay, this is really going to happen! My anxiety seemed to loosen a little, and the miscarriages started to slip into ancient history. I didn't need to actually *make* a baby. Our baby was already waiting for us in China.

Chapter 9

The Shortcut

NOVEMBER 2000

I was sure our baby was waiting for us in China, so now I needed to find the right agency to help us bring her home. I was ready to be a mom *now* and I was sure someone out there could help us find her right away. I would make as many calls as needed to find the agency with the right program and connections to get my Chinese baby home quickly.

The very first workshop we attended was held right in the town next to us at the library. It was an informational lecture, basically, about a local agency that does both domestic adoptions and international adoptions through China. Luckily, it was scheduled for just a couple of days after I had done my marathon internet search, so I had a lot of interest and momentum going into the evening.

We got to the modern community library with a wall full of posters at the entrance. A sign boasted a large arrow pointing to a meeting room. The room, which was usually a pretty bland conference room with plain white walls and gray industrial carpet, had been decorated with beautiful artifacts from China, including a huge red paper dragon that looked a bit like a piñata, and a beautiful creamy white silk robe with intricate embroidery hung on the wall. At the front of the room sat a screen and projector, and about half of the chairs were filled with couples who looked as nervous as we felt.

The meeting went well enough. We got some basic information about the China program, confirmed for ourselves that we had no interest in even gathering information about domestic programs, and began to get a flavor of what it might be like to travel to China. It all felt surreal but exciting. This was our first exposure to this world, and I felt just a bit scared and overwhelmed. China is very far away and a completely different culture from ours. Less than a week ago we were sure our travels for this baby wouldn't extend any farther than the hospital in downtown Chicago.

The program sounded okay, but the wait time seemed endless. The agency was quoting a total of almost two years before we would be able to bring home our baby. That sounded like an eternity to me. I knew times to complete an adoption varied greatly. Although it does vary by country, it also varies by agency, how long it takes the family to gather all of the necessary paperwork, and also some random things like timing of holidays and sometimes just luck. Two years was a reasonably average time for a Chinese adoption, but I couldn't possibly consider waiting so long. As I mentally crossed this agency off the list, assuming I could find one that could get through the process faster, I began to relax and listen to the presentation, drinking in the information.

As we walked to our car Marc said, "This agency seems so nice. They are close by, and they travel in large groups of families, so we'd have companions...."

Once the car doors were closed, I said, "Yeah, whatever, we're not using them." He looked at me, puzzled, and I succinctly explained, "I'm not waiting two years for a baby. If those other people want to wait that long, that is their problem!"

Of course, Marc saw things quite differently from me. He thought it seemed like an interesting presentation and an agency we should pursue. He had the darn logical attitude that the Chinese government had a very strict program and closely followed prescription for how to adopt a baby. Now, even though I had been told this many times by many people, for some reason, I was still convinced there must be another way. We didn't really fight about it, but I could see in Marc's eyes he was thinking, *Here we go again!*

He was right, of course. I spent many hours over the next several days talking with different agencies about their Chinese adoption programs. I had lots of questions about the protocol, timeline, fees, and dossier requirements. Basically, I expected the person I got on the phone for each agency to give me every detail.

I had been trying to reach one specific agency to find out about their program. I believe they had a spreadsheet on their website that listed the wait time for their China program as much shorter than I was hearing from other agencies. Of course I was itching to talk to someone there, so I had made several calls. But each time, the person who could answer my numerous questions was unavailable.

I was still attending graduate school at this time, and I remember the night I was at school, sitting in a messy and crowded classroom, when the woman I needed to speak with called me back. The lecture on narcissism had just begun when my phone chimed loudly, and I tried to slip out of class without making a scene. Unfortunately, I am not the most graceful person and knocked over multiple books, backpacks, and winter coats as I made my way to the door.

I eventually got to the student lounge where I curled up on a sofa with my notepad while this lady patiently answered all of my questions. I sat there through my entire class and long past the time the rest of my classmates went home. I had several pages of notes, but they were in no way related to personality disorders.

I was getting extremely frustrated at this point, because these agencies were not telling me what I wanted to hear. Although some were more than happy to help me get my dossier together quickly, they all said the same thing about the rest of the process. The Chinese government has one single protocol for any families who want to adopt, regardless of the agency they are using. If the diplomats in China are taking eighteen to twenty-four months to go through paperwork and assign referrals, that is simply how long it takes.

I refused to accept this. I am a very logical person, and I figured if it takes nine months to have a baby, that is how long it should take to have a baby. If I couldn't carry one myself, I should be able to adopt one within nine months. I'm not sure exactly how I came to this conclusion, but I was holding fast to it.

I was hoping to do a better job than anyone else and actually get a baby in much less than nine months. I wanted to show the world how on top of things I was. Like I was saying to fate, "You don't want to let me be pregnant? That is just fine. I didn't want to wait that whole nine months to be a mother, anyway." I didn't tell anyone this was my attitude. In fact, I'm not sure I was totally aware of it even myself. But I was certainly aware I was not willing to wait another two years before I could say I was a mom.

It was like a quest for the most fabulous coupon or clearance sale. I would beat the system. I was going to have a child, and it certainly wasn't going to take as long as everyone else was willing to wait. I would find the shortcut or back door that would allow me to get this done ASAP.

Eventually, after several of these lengthy phone calls, I spoke to a woman who worked for an agency in Utah. She was extremely nice, and I really enjoyed talking with her. She corroborated the rest of the industry's claim that adopting from China really would take at least two years. However, unlike the other agencies who just got frustrated from my endless questions and insistence that there must be a quicker path, she actually presented a solution. She asked if I had considered adopting from Vietnam.

In fact, up to that point I had *not* considered this alternative. I didn't know anyone who had adopted from Vietnam, and I knew nothing about the laws or process there. Of course, as an American, I had a gut reaction about even the word "Vietnam" and thought back to the war. So I had not even been aware that a Vietnamese adoption was something available to me.

Micki, the representative of the Utah agency who became a close friend in the years to come, said she really liked the Vietnamese program. Micki was exactly the type of person I enjoyed working with. She was very kind but also direct. She wasn't going to give me a timeline or expectation that wasn't reliable.

I learned later that Micki is not only professional and great to work with, but she is truly a remarkable woman with a huge and wonderful family. She has eight incredible children—four of whom are adopted and diverse in race as well as interests and abilities. They are a beautiful and loving family, and Micki is one of the most amazing and most genuine people I have ever met. I trusted her completely and still do.

Micki explained while China has a very rigid, national process that all adoptive families go through, Vietnam does not. Each province in Vietnam has its own laws for adoptions, just like each state in the US does. The waiting period, method for terminating parental rights, and even the paperwork required are totally different for each of the fifty states. The same is true in Vietnam. Some provinces even require only one versus two trips to the country for the family wanting to adopt, and the necessary paperwork, requirements, and abandonment procedures vary greatly depending upon the province where the baby is located. This makes adopting from Vietnam a much more flexible, if less predictable, process.

Well, this was the loophole I had been looking for! I probed further and inhaled every speck of information Micki gave me about Vietnamese adoptions. If we went through the right province, the process could be quicker, the children available younger, and it was even possible at times to meet the birth mother while traveling to pick up the child. What more could I ask for? It was perfect!

Micki was the angel I had been looking for. I traded in my roadmap and shifted gears again. It was time to learn everything I could about Vietnam.

Chapter 10

Good Morning, Vietnam!

NOVEMBER 2000

Good morning, Vietnam!

After learning all about adopting from China, I now changed my focus to finding all the different agencies that had programs in Vietnam. Marc didn't have much of a problem with the change in countries, but of course, he asked me about a million questions. He wanted to know all the details and particulars about the process, timeline, and requirements for adopting from Vietnam. He asked for specific comparisons between China and Vietnam besides just the fact that it would be a much quicker process to go to Vietnam.

As I found and contacted several agencies who had Vietnamese programs, I could immediately see the difference between adopting from the two different countries.

The details and answers to questions were extremely consistent among agencies when asking about their China programs. Of course, some traveled with large groups and others didn't, some had many guides traveling with the families and some had only one guide or facilitator. The agencies often preferred different hotels or travel agencies in different regions of China. But basically, the process didn't differ much at all between all the Chinese programs I inquired about, regardless of the agency. For each one, I would need to put together a dossier of the same length, and then the process for submitting the paperwork to China was consistently the same. I would receive a referral after a similar number of weeks, and the length of the trip to China was about the same number of days. The fees varied slightly as well between agencies, but again were all within a few thousand dollars without exception. Most importantly to me, the timeline quoted was always about the same. It would take about two years to adopt from China. In other words, endless.

I now know there is a good reason for this. The Chinese government has very specific guidelines for adopting a child from their country. Every single adoption petition goes through the central government of the country, and the process is the same for each and every one. If petitions are filed from three different agencies on the same day, those petitions will each be honored in the same way, and the referrals will be handed out in the order the petitions are received. This is why I was unable to find an agency that would be able to help me adopt from China in a shorter period of time. It was completely out of their control. The central Chinese government held total control of every aspect of the process from the time the petition was filed.

In Vietnam, however, the situation was very different. Because the provinces each control their own rules and regulations, they are vastly different. Further, different agencies have relationships and agreements with specific orphanages. So, the families who adopt through China may travel to any part of the country to get their child, regardless of the agency they are working with. Families who adopt from Vietnam may know which orphanage, and consequently which province, their child will come from even before their paperwork is filed. Other agencies may go to one of several different orphanages. However, each agency works with only a few orphanages, so families know they will be going to one of those specific places.

Because of this, the answers to my list of questions were very different for every agency I called about their Vietnam program. Some of them would know that the process might take six to eight months and the family would be required to go on two trips of one week each. This is because those were the rules for the specific province where the only orphanage that agency worked with was located.

Another agency might give a huge range of time for the wait before referral because they work with orphanages in many different provinces and get referrals from all of them. The costs, timelines, and specifics varied so greatly it was much more difficult to compare the programs and agencies than it was when I was inquiring about Chinese programs. So, in some cases, it was necessary to compare and make a decision about the province I wanted to adopt from as well as the agency I wanted to use.

Being as driven as I was, I focused on the programs who said they could possibly have the shortest total time between submitting the paperwork and actually taking placement of a child. I made spreadsheets organizing the time from dossier submission to referral, time from referral to travel, total time we would be required to travel, and combined time to placement.

After making comparisons, I was able to narrow the field to two possible agencies. The total time until I would have my child for the two was pretty comparable, and it was shorter than the other programs I had gathered information about.

I had a tough time deciding between the two programs, though.

Micki's agency in Utah, who first told me about adopting from Vietnam, was one of my two favorites. Micki was their director for all Asian adoptions. I liked her so much, and the agency seemed very friendly and quaint. I felt I would receive personal attention from them but had some concerns about using an agency that was so small. I was also a little apprehensive about the fact they were so far away from me. Micki told me it didn't make a difference where they were located, but Utah felt very remote and different from the Chicago area where I lived.

The second agency I liked was not geographically close either. They were located in Virginia. It was almost as far away as Utah, but they had one coordinator who was actually living in the Chicago area. Even though she did not work on the Vietnam program, I found it comforting to have a local representative. I was actually able to meet her in person. This meant I was able to talk with her face-to-face and learn general information about the agency.

Also, it was a very large agency who did a large number of adoptions each year from several different countries. They had stressed to me the value of this because if there was some reason we might want to change countries, we would be able to switch programs within the agency with little hassle or loss of funds. Although I didn't like anyone in particular at the agency as much as I did Micki, I finally decided it was the safer choice. I told Micki, and she was completely supportive, telling me, "Just follow your gut. You need to do what feels best to you."

Marc and I attended many educational seminars and workshops on the weekends from the time we first made the decision to adopt. One of the requirements for our home study was completing a certain number of educational hours about adoption, and we were also eager to learn everything we could.

The very first seminar we went to at the library gave us a general overview of the adoption process. We later attended workshops about emotional difficulties specific to adoptees, general health risks when traveling abroad—both for us and the children from other countries—specific activities with a group called "families with children from Vietnam" that focused on Vietnamese culture, as well as general parenting classes like infant CPR.

We attended a three-day intensive adoption convention with classes where we could learn all about adoption, and we got to watch interviews with panels of adoptees, their adoptive parents, and even their birth parents.

While I had been gathering the information and comparing different countries and then agencies, I also had made note of every possible educational opportunity in our area. Anything that came up about any aspect of adoption went immediately on our calendar. By the time we actually selected our agency, we had learned as much as we could about international adoption.

At the various seminars we were able to meet many professionals. These included adoption attorneys, pediatricians who specialized in children adopted from other countries, parents who had already successfully completed adoptions, adoptees, birth mothers, and workers from many adoption agencies. Marc also liked the woman from the Virginia agency we met at a seminar.

So, after hours and hours of phone calls and discussions with Marc, I relayed our decision to the home study worker.

She recorded our choice of agency and listed Vietnam as the country we'd be traveling to, adding these details to the plethora of facts she had already gathered about us.

Was it almost done yet? I couldn't wait for the home study to be finished because it was the biggest part of our dossier and the part I had the least amount of control over when it could be completed. My baby was getting closer. I could just feel it in my bones!

Chapter 11

Skeletons in the Closet

———

Ugh! Does she want to rifle through my underwear drawer too?

The ordeal of completing a home study was only slightly less stress-provoking than that of choosing an agency. The first step was selecting who would actually write the home study. I made the same litany of phone calls to organizations who wrote home studies in our area I had initially made when comparing Chinese programs. The results were quite comparable.

The home study process was pretty consistent regardless of who was writing it. I found some discrepancies between the cost and length of time it would take to complete the home study, however. Of course, I immediately chose the agency who told me they would be able to complete mine in the shortest amount of time.

This agency said it would take four to six weeks to have the home study written if I could get my paperwork done as quickly as possible. Since this was the best offer I received, I made an appointment to get started on the first possible date the agency could send someone out.

The first visit from our home study worker would be several hours long. Of course, I had been very anxious about it and had cleaned the house from top to bottom. Marc and I ate dinner early that night, and I baked homemade muffins for the occasion. When the home study woman arrived, the three of us sat down on the antique love seat and mahogany club chairs that flanked the fireplace in our formal living room. The muffins provided a wonderful aroma, and the house was more immaculate than it had been since we'd lived there.

Marc and I answered what seemed like hundreds of questions. Some were easy, of course, like the basic facts. We cheerfully told this woman our wedding date and location, general information about the families we grew up in, and more objective facts than we ever thought could be relevant. It was like filling out an extremely long and general questionnaire or survey about every aspect of our lives.

After the extensive, initial, "survey" period of the interview, many of the questions became much less specific and more difficult to answer. We were pretty unprepared for questions like, "How do you want to parent your child? What general philosophy will you use to guide your parenting decisions? How will your relationship as a couple change and grow with the addition of a child? What will you do to remain close as a couple? How will you discipline a child? How will you incorporate the child's culture and religion of birth into your family?" These are just a small sampling of the inquiries made of us as we stared at the social worker with open mouths.

We did some quick and silent soul-searching (or at least I did) to answer these questions in a consistent manner and as honestly as we possibly could. It should look like we've already discussed this at length. Right? Does everyone talk extensively about how they're going to handle a child who colors on the wall before they decide to get pregnant?

After our meeting I remember feeling a little offended at the sheer number and depth of questions we were expected to have ready answers for. It didn't seem fair that no one is expected to provide a single bit of information or proof that they can be good parents before getting pregnant. They didn't have to prove even the basics of a place to live, employment, or family support to bring their child home from the hospital. Of course not, it's their child! While I understand the importance of making sure adoptive parents are physically and financially able to care for a child, the intense interrogation seemed excessive.

At the time, we were trying to impress this woman and get through the evening, so we trudged through the invasive queries and did our best to give the "right" answers to the litany of questions. Of course we easily agreed that we would never hit our child, and also that we would do everything we could to celebrate all aspects of the culture we were adopting from along with the child. We were asked further specifics like how we would discipline in general and we muddled our way through the answers. I tried to think back to the specifics of the parenting course I taught for clues on this, and did my best to send mental signals to Marc about the appropriate techniques and strategies.

Some additional topics fell somewhere in the middle as far as difficulty for us. Fortunately, we were both born into the same religion and both practiced in similar ways. We were very much attached to the customs of our religion, if not the actual spiritual aspects. Our friends and family could all report favorably on the traditional Passover Seder we host every spring, complete with gummy frogs and marshmallows representing the ten plagues. Our menorah and candles for Chanukah were already on display since it was coming up in just a few weeks. I'm sure other couples may have had more difficulty in this area, but we were proud of our ability to tackle this section so proficiently.

We also felt pretty competent when discussing our own families of origin. We explained what it was like to grow up in our community (our childhood homes and our home at the time were all located within about a mile of each other) and further within our own families. We were able to get through the description of our own parents' parenting style, and also our current and ongoing relationships and contact with our extended families.

I know we covered a multitude of other topics that night, but these were the highlights in my mind. When we were finished with our examination, we were handed our lengthy homework assignment. The list of paperwork we would need to collect was quite daunting. I could see I was going to put a lot of miles on my car gathering everything we would need.

The list of documents I was expected to collect was nothing short of overwhelming. The home study woman said it would likely take about one to two months to gather everything necessary. Of course, I took this as a challenge and began immediately! This project was like a scavenger hunt. I would win and collect these thirty-five random items faster than anyone.

Several of the items needed to be procured from out of state, and we had many hoops to jump through in order to collect those, requiring the acquisition and notarization of a whole new set of documents. It should have been made into a game show!

One example of an "added level of difficulty" item was the police report showing we had not committed any crimes. It sounded easy until I learned that I'd need to bring a notary with me to the police station.

In an attempt to preserve Marc's cooperation and enthusiasm for the project, I did most of the legwork on my own, only enlisting his help as needed. No matter how hard I tried, I knew I couldn't get our family physician to sign off on Marc's required physical form without Marc actually coming to his office, so that would definitely be on the list of things I would ask for him to get done promptly.

Along with the documents I collected on the scavenger hunt, extensive forms needed to be completed. I filled out all of them, using sticky notes to indicate where Marc should sign.

Even with the items I needed Marc's help for, I had everything on the required list within a week's time. I knew I must have won this race!

I gathered everything in a large envelope and delivered the entire package to the office of the home study agency. Normally families would just mail it in, but I wanted to hand-deliver everything so I wouldn't lose an extra day or two by putting it in the mail.

When I arrived to deliver our package of documents, our home study worker was at her desk, so I proudly presented it to her in person. In contrast to my efficiency, she was very nonchalant and informed me she hadn't even started our report yet. This was who I had chosen as a partner in this race?

She told us she had made it clear she wouldn't be able to get much done until she had all of the supporting paperwork required in hand. When I indicated to her that every document requested was located in the envelope I had given her, she didn't quite believe me. I guess it usually takes much longer before anyone is able to complete the entire assignment. She had underestimated my level of motivation, but she didn't seem adequately impressed. She told me she would get to it soon and would contact me when she had made some progress.

With my leg of the race complete, I couldn't do anything more in the coming weeks to expedite things any further. This was my first introduction to the endless waiting game involved in adoption. I had been feverishly running around for a week, and now I was put on hold. I longed for another project.

Chapter 12

Dossier=More Paperwork

NOVEMBER–DECEMBER 2000

Once the baton was passed back to me in the form of a completed home study, I would be ready to run. I didn't yet realize I had only completed a very short sprint at the beginning of this marathon.

I knew I would need to compile a dossier. This was another, even larger packet of paperwork and documents required for the country of Vietnam. Each country had their own dossier with its own list of necessary paperwork. Some were standard items for the country of Vietnam, and then additional items were required based upon the province.

The home study and all of the supporting documents I had collected were included in this packet, but I had to procure multiple additional items and forms (in Vietnamese!) that required our signatures. After I gathered everything on our list, the entire thing needed to be notarized (if it hadn't been already), and then each document would receive a state seal, which could be obtained only from one of two offices in the whole state. After the seals were affixed, I would send the precious packet down to the Vietnamese Embassy in

Washington, DC, where they would translate every item into Vietnamese before returning it to me.

Simultaneously, we would have to apply for approval from the INS. In order to bring a child home to the US, we needed to have the proper immigration status. However, this application also required a copy of our completed home study.

When we received the Vietnamese-translated version of our dossier *and* the approval from INS, our agency could finally submit our application by sending all of this stuff over to Vietnam to be matched with a child. Only then would we receive our "referral" and get specific details about our child, the travel we would complete, and the date everything could be done.

So, the bottom line was, I was kind of stuck on hold until this home study was completed.

I tried to wait patiently and made sure I had everything else I would need. All systems were go, and everything was ready and waiting for this one single document.

When the home study worker called to say that we should set up our next meeting, I was more than ready. I wanted her to come as quickly as she possibly could. We set up a meeting, and she let me know it would be much shorter than the last one.

When she arrived, we went over our list and confirmed she had everything she needed from our end. She showed us some of the report she had already completed and asked a few questions to tie up loose ends she had overlooked the first time. It seemed quick and easy, and I was sure she was going to tell me the report would be completed the next day.

She told us we just needed to fill in a few small items. I assured her I would have any additional information to her the following day and she should plan on getting our home study done as soon as possible. She got offended and said she had always told us it would take up to six weeks, and she wasn't even close to that deadline yet. I thought this was quite unreasonable, given the efficiency with which I had completed my assignment for this project. She was not the team player I had hoped she would be. I wanted her to call me the minute the home study was finished so I could pick it up immediately.

The day I finally heard that our home study was complete was just short of the full six weeks they had quoted me. I was tempted to complain, but by that time I just wanted to get it in my hands and move forward! I rushed to the office, got my copies, and organized everything in my car. I then sped down to downtown Chicago where the immigration office was located.

After going through a metal detector, I entered the cavernous INS office, where I had to literally take a number. I then sat in a huge room of folding chairs, mostly filled by about twenty-five people who all appeared to be of foreign descent. Employees peered through a hole in plexiglass windows along one wall to call out numbers. The walls were all plain white cinderblocks, adorned only with a few random flyers. I sat quietly in the uncomfortable metal seat, listening to bits and pieces of conversations in a multitude of languages.

When my number was finally called, I went to the window with my packet of paperwork. The woman behind the glass looked at me, confused. I explained that I needed to submit this for approval. "Why didn't you just mail it in like every other adopting family?" she asked.

"I guess I'm not like everyone else who wants to adopt. I want this taken care of as quickly as possible," I tried to explain.

She just shook her head and gave me an odd look. "We will contact you *by mail* to request any additional items or to inform you when your application has been approved." I felt only slightly foolish for making the extra effort but was content that nothing could be lost in the mail, and maybe I had saved myself an extra day or so by not relying on the postal service.

I then fought morning traffic and my bad sense of direction through downtown Chicago. I have lived in the suburbs my whole life, but despite being only a short drive away from the city of Chicago, I rarely visit.

I was relieved when I found the towering office building where I could get the state seals and then even more relieved when I procured an actual legal parking spot—no easy feat in this location!

The office was much less sparse than the one for INS, but I again had to take a number and wait. Who knew that places other than the deli actually used numbers? The desk where employees called numbers from was made of wood without plexiglass windows. Some artwork even adorned the walls, and the chairs were different too, actual upholstered furniture with slightly textured hunter green fabric. I couldn't help but think I was in the home stretch!

By the time my number was called, the state worker I spoke with informed me they would be going on their lunch break in just ten minutes. I should leave my packet and I could return in about two hours to retrieve it, or they could mail it to me. While I was exhausted, I was certainly not willing to lose another business day or two waiting for the mail. Besides, how could I ensure it wouldn't get lost? I would be back for my packet that afternoon as soon as it was ready.

When I reached the lobby, I first called Marc to inform him we would be having a lunch date since I was not far from his office. I then called my horse trainer to let him know I would be neglecting my steed yet another day. I supposed he should get used to seeing me more infrequently. After all, I was going to be a mom soon!

I entered the loud New York-style deli with wings on my feet. I found Marc sitting at a table in the corner which was covered with a checkered tablecloth with two sandwiches and Diet Cokes already laid out for us. I was starving and grateful, feeling tired but extremely proud of the progress I had made. I was sure no one could have gotten these tasks done any faster, and I was patting myself on the back, confident everything would go smoothly now that we had cleared the home study hurdle.

Somehow, Marc didn't share my elation. "We still need the embassy to translate everything," Marc quietly reminded me as he unwrapped his fork from a paper napkin. I began to deflate a bit. Marc was always my voice of reason and grounding.

"It might take several weeks, and you know it may not be done by Tet," he continued to throw cold water on my good mood. The Vietnamese New Year, Tet, was coming up in February, and the entire government of Vietnam takes off to celebrate for pretty much the whole month.

"It's already December, so if they don't finish before the holiday, our stuff won't be done until March," he went on as I devoured my pastrami sandwich. "Even if they get it done, we probably won't be able to get it over to Vietnam before Tet, so the holiday will delay our match and referral on that end."

I refused to let him bring me down. Marc is somewhat of a pessimist; he always likes to plan for the worst, but I was not going to let him interfere with my fantasies. I was sure everything now would be done in the shortest possible time. It was a happy day. "Don't worry." I smiled. "Everything is going to proceed smoothly. I'm on it! We're going to bring that baby home before you know it!"

He looked at me skeptically and ate his lunch as he allowed me to go on and on about what had become "imaginary baby."

Marc realized long ago that the easiest way to deal with me was to go along with my whims instead of arguing with me. He even took off the rest of the afternoon to help me. He seemed to recognize my need to get as much as possible done this very minute, even if he didn't think it would make any difference.

Marc drove me back to the state building and waited in the car while I ran up to gather the precious fruits of my labor. He then watched as I carefully arranged the sheets of paper in the Federal Express envelope I had already lovingly prepared. He drove me to a post office where I could personally deposit the envelope into the FedEx box and wish it well for the next leg of its journey.

I felt a renewed energy. While Marc was trying to keep my expectations in check, he was starting to show the slightest signs of actually being excited that this would happen. I was thrilled to have him on board and a more active participant in our "imaginary baby" project. We could tackle the next step even better if we worked together.

Chapter 13

Gammy's Gone

DECEMBER 2000

My life had become the adoption process, or the adoption process had become my life. I'm not sure which, but my entire life was now laser-focused in a single direction—on finding my baby. I had either eliminated or minimized the attention I paid to my friends, school, riding, and everything else in my world. That bubble I created around me of all things baby and adoption was burst on a cold day in December when devastating news from my family forced my attention away from my own quest for a child.

Now that the paperwork had been sent to the embassy, we couldn't do anything more on the adoption front but wait. I was sure the months of December and January were going to move very slowly despite the holidays. I would try to distract myself and remember, if I had anything to do with it, we would be celebrating our holidays the following year with our child.

Unfortunately, it did not turn out for me to have a boring month in December of 2000. My grandmother passed away shortly after I sent my paperwork to Washington, DC.

"Gammy," as I called her, had been a shining star of my life. Since I was an infant, she was my fairy godmother, my soft place to fall. From the day I was born until the day she died, she referred to me as "her number one grandchild," and she treated me as such. This was the stem of much of my self-esteem and self-image.

Although my mother and I had a fairly volatile relationship and hadn't even spoken much for a couple of years, I always had her mother on my side. Most of my family stood behind my mother without even wanting to hear how I felt about things. But Gammy listened to everything I had to say. She never told me I was wrong or made me feel guilty. She understood why I needed to stay separate from my mother, and she respected that. I loved her dearly and will miss her for the rest of my life.

Gammy was a tiny woman, but her huge heart and personality filled every room she entered. She was about five feet tall and wore a halo of blonde that was lovingly created by Dino, her hairdresser, every Saturday morning at ten. She was the quintessential Jewish grandma, loving to everyone and only wanting all of our happiness.

Gammy had gotten sick earlier in the fall. She had difficulty breathing and was admitted to the hospital and put on a respirator. She had become dependent on it but appeared to be getting better. All reports of her condition described a plan for weaning her from the machine. We had no indication her condition was expected to be fatal, and she really seemed to be making constant improvement.

Because of the respirator, however, she was unable to talk on the phone. I spoke with her nurses regularly and checked on her condition. Sometimes they would hold the phone to her ear so she could hear my voice. I hoped to go and visit her that fall, but the logistics were difficult.

I fully believed my gammy would get better, so I decided to wait to go visit until one of two things happened. First, if she were able to get off of the respirator and really talk to me, I would go see her right away. Even if she didn't, however, I planned to go as soon as I had some concrete facts about the child I would be adopting.

I knew having a great-grandchild would mean the world to Gammy. She adored babies and would have been happier than anyone, including me, to know about becoming a "great-gammy." I was sure I would get a referral and be able to bring her a photo of the baby that would soon be ours. I felt strongly this would give her a new lease on life and even a reason for living and fighting to get better.

Gammy was one of the few people I had told about my first miscarriage, and we discussed it at length. But by the time of the second one, she was already in the hospital. She was so incredibly excited about the idea that I was going to be a mom, and I had a beautiful vision of what it would be like to show her an actual photo of my first child. It was what I was most looking forward to, even more than getting the picture and information for myself.

I never got to show Gammy a photo of my first child—or of my second or third children, for that matter. She developed an infection from being in the hospital and rapidly went into a coma. Within days, she was gone. My trip to Philadelphia was for her funeral rather than her rebirth.

It was one of the saddest times of my life. I couldn't believe she was gone, and I felt a loneliness and sadness I had never before experienced. I remember thinking so many times that week of all the things I wanted to tell her. I was at peace in knowing she truly understood how much I loved her and how much she meant to me. I just couldn't imagine not being able to call her and tell her about all of my feelings and adventures. Her warm approval and unconditional love made everything I went through in life more real and more special.

Now I would have to get through the rest of my life without her. I would have to raise my kids without ever asking her advice or being able to share with her all of their accomplishments. She would never know them or even see their faces. I knew in advance how much love she would have for them and how much they would have had for her.

I knew from that point on, I would live the rest of my life for both myself and for Gammy. Every day I try to be as good a person as she was and as she would want me to be. I try to tell my kids the things she told me when I was sad that made everything all right. I feel her spirit lives on in my children; that they are somehow a continuation of the loving, spunky woman she was. They are my new guardian angels and soft place to fall.

I traveled to Philadelphia for her funeral, and while I was there, I saw dozens of relatives I hadn't seen in years. The Jewish tradition requires the family to "sit Shiva." I don't know exactly what the scriptures mandate, but I know what it looks like in practice.

The immediate family opens their home to any family and friends who want to come by to pay respects. They all bring or send food. The trays of bagel and lox, sandwich meats, pastries, cookies, and more can be excessive. Everyone sits around chatting and eating, sometimes for just a few hours after the funeral and sometimes for several days.

We all went to my uncle's house after the funeral, where the trays of food were waiting for us. We sat around his dining room and living room catching up, and many people asked if I was having a baby. Gammy shared with my family that I was considering having children without revealing any details or disclosing anything she thought I may want to keep secret.

I dodged the questions for a while but eventually decided I should share the plans for our future child with my family. I broke to them the news that I had wanted to share with Gammy. I told them all about our planned adoption and trip to Vietnam. The whole family was together, so I was able to share with everyone and answer questions all at once.

Everyone was interested and listened to me politely, asking questions and offering congratulations. But it was painfully clear to me that no one would have even close to the reaction I would have gotten from my gammy—the simple joy and elation I know without question she would have had. I was glad to have shared our news, but at the same time, I felt an emptiness from that too. There was no one in the rest of my family with whom I had nearly the relationship I had with Gammy, and no one stepped up to fill that spot for me.

In retrospect, none of this should have surprised me. I knew no aunt or cousin could ever fill the spot Gammy held. It may have been better for me if I had just kept my mouth shut and then I could at least hold on to the secret that was meant to be shared with Gammy before anyone else. But I don't keep secrets well, and I acted consistently with how I felt that day.

I would never have the moment I had dreamed of sharing with Gammy, and I am sorry for that. However, the love I now feel for my children has matched the close bond I had as a child with Gammy. Knowing this relationship and closeness from the other, adult side is something I didn't know I would ever do and has only heightened the appreciation I still hold for the special bond Gammy and I shared.

If I ever questioned my decision to have a baby, this experience of loss extinguished any doubts. It reminded me of the power and value of the connection between generations. I was proud to be continuing this line of my family and would always tell my child of the beautiful Gammy she almost got to meet.

Now I had my grief to focus on while I waited to meet my child for the first time. But I would soon get shocking news that would cut this grieving time short.

Chapter 14

I'm Going to Vietnam

JANUARY 2001

My surprise was genuine when the next unexpected call left me in tears of joy instead of grief.

I had been anxiously watching the calendar and measuring the passing days and weeks against the estimated time for our dossier to be translated. I wanted to wait until at least the early end of the estimate before I called our agency to needlessly question if they had heard anything. You know, six to eight weeks *could* mean six weeks, or even five and a half. Right?

I was in the warm family room of my sister-in-law Joan's house just four weeks after I had sent in my dossier for translation. It was a cold winter day, and I had tried to distract myself from the adoption "waiting game" by stopping at Joan's place for a visit. It was almost lunchtime, and Joan graciously threw together a lovely spread of salad, smoked salmon, and fruit. We were sipping tea after lunch, sitting on the comfortable brown leather sectional sofa that faced Joan's brick fireplace, and she was trying to convince me to be patient. Just as we got up to clear the dishes, my cell phone rang.

It was the woman from my agency. When I recognized the caller ID, I picked up the phone in excitement, hoping for news but honestly expecting a silly question or meaningless update without any actual new information.

"We got word that your dossier translation is complete," the voice on the phone said, and I couldn't stop the huge grin from spreading across my face. "It is being FedExed today from the embassy, and we should have it back tomorrow," she continued since I couldn't really find my voice.

I was beside myself now, grinning from ear to ear and clutching the side of the brown sofa to keep myself steady. We were one step closer to our child. Before I had truly registered this information, though, she went on.

"Would you be able to travel to Vietnam twice instead of once?" she asked.

I wasn't quite sure how to answer this. We had chosen this agency in part because we would only have to travel once. My face fell as I told her, "There is no way my husband can take off of work twice."

"No problem," the voice told me cheerfully. "Only one parent needs to travel on the first trip to submit the paperwork. Both parents are only required for the second trip to attend the giving and receiving ceremony and bring your child home." I knew this was the final step of the adoption process, when all of the paperwork was neatly in order. The facilitator, orphanage representative, adopting family, and even sometimes the birth mother participated in a ceremonial "giving and receiving" ritual to pass custody of the child to her new family.

I was absolutely terrified of traveling anywhere at all alone. I didn't even go to a horse show a two-hour drive from home on my own. I always begged Marc to come with me if I didn't have a friend I was attending the show with. I must have been really invested in the idea of having a child, because I surprised myself by responding, "Well, I guess that will be okay then." What was I thinking? I'm sure I hadn't even considered or recognized I would be flying to a foreign, communist country on the other side of the globe by myself.

I asked why it would be necessary for me to travel twice. She explained they previously had a relationship with an orphanage in a province named Thai Nguyen, and the laws for that province only require a family to make one trip to Vietnam. Basically, the dossier is allowed to be submitted by mail and then the family travels only to take placement of the child.

Earlier in the week, however, this orphanage made a decision to suspend any adoptions to the United States. The INS recently started requiring more paperwork, and this orphanage decided they weren't willing to go through these extra steps most other countries did not require. I asked if there were other orphanages in that province, and she explained she didn't know how long it would be before the agency would be able to develop a working agreement with another orphanage.

They were currently working with two other orphanages in two other provinces, both of which required the family to make two trips to Vietnam. I agreed if it was going to be my quickest option—with no actual time estimate for the other—I could manage to make the first trip myself and return with Marc the following month.

The next exchange literally took my breath away. She asked, "Well, would you be able to go next week?" I must have almost collapsed or turned white or something because

Joan came over, put her hand on my shoulder, and asked if I was okay. From that point on, I was a little flustered.

I learned a baby girl was available in Lang Son province, and her name was Viet. Her photo was being emailed to me as soon as I accepted the referral.

My hands shook as I hung up the phone, and before I could say a word, Joan smiled at me and said, "Congratulations." She has a knack for skipping unnecessary words and getting immediately to the point.

I ran upstairs to use her computer as I dialed Marc's number on my cell phone. Marc was excited but skeptical as always. Of course, he wanted to know all the details of the situation, about the provinces, the different orphanages, the differences in paperwork, and travel requirements.

I got a little frustrated with his endless questioning because I couldn't even focus. I could remember little of the previous phone conversation besides the one single statement that mattered: "There is a little girl available for you." Eventually, he gave up trying to gather any more information from me and said, "I'll just call the agency myself to get all the details." Probably a good plan. I was pretty much speechless and not a big help just then.

Marc was on the job now. He printed out the photos for me and said he would let his boss know he would be gone the following month to travel overseas. He called the agency and got all the information we would need.

I had hoped to have a friend travel with me, but it's not so easy to find someone who can just take off for a week with no notice and who also has a valid passport and willing spirit.

I asked my friend Tammy to come with me. I met Tammy at the beginning of seventh grade, a wiry Asian girl with round tortoise-shell glasses over her playful brown eyes, and she instantly became my best friend. She had grown into a beautiful woman, still thin but now filled out with dark hair she kept in a bob cut, and the glasses were now gone. But Tammy had never ceased to be the "sister" I had never had and my go-to best friend in all emergencies. Tammy would have come with me if she could, but my flight was leaving in a matter of days and her passport was expired. Nothing could be done in time. I had to face the reality I would be making this trip by myself.

For the next week I was on the phone almost constantly with the woman at our agency as I tried to prepare for the trip. I got all the paperwork I needed, received my expedited visa, and did a lot of shopping.

I already purchased two enormous duffel bags on wheels in preparation for the long trip I thought I would be taking with Marc. Now I learned what I would need to pack for myself to spend a week in Vietnam, and also which things I'd need to bring for the baby. Not only would I need to bring a month's worth of clothes, cloth diapers, blankets and other supplies for baby Viet, but it was expected for me to gather a huge amount of similar items to leave at the orphanage as a donation. By the time the week was up, my duffels were stuffed so full they looked like a person could be hidden inside.

Many times since receiving that call at Joan's house, I reached out to the agency panicking about some aspect of the trip. Each time the same sweet voice on the phone calmed me down and did her best to answer my questions. My biggest concern was I would be traveling alone and would not know what to do or how to get around.

I learned that the agency had rushed my referral through because doing so would time my trip to be able to travel with two other women who were also adopting from the same province. They were both single women, and their trip was scheduled to be a few days off from mine, but with a little arm-twisting and maneuvering, the agency was able to adjust the timing. I would be arriving in Vietnam a couple of days later than the other women, but we would all come back to the US at the same time.

Both of these women had planned to adopt from Lang Son, making the two trips, so they had to be there a little earlier to get some of the approvals on their paperwork that had already been done for mine in Washington, DC. They did not know each other either.

One woman, Pat, would be traveling with her mother, and the other, Jan, would be by herself, just like me. We were coming from three different parts of the country, so we would each make the approximately twenty-four-hour journey—just the time in the air—on our own, but once we got to Vietnam, we would be able to lean on each other and have support through the trip.

At my request through the agency, I got a call that night from Jan, who would be traveling alone to Hanoi from North Carolina. Jan had a sweet Southern accent and seemed almost as frazzled as I felt. We were able to compare notes, which was extremely helpful and calming for both of us. She gathered some details from the agency that I had missed, and vice versa. In general, we both felt good about having someone else in the same boat.

Jan was all packed and would be flying in just a couple of days. She had not yet talked with the third woman traveling, and since she was leaving first, I think she was possibly even more grateful than I was to have been able to touch base with one of her traveling partners before she left.

I was relieved she would be able to get the lay of the land before I got there and would be waiting for me. I think this was the point when I finally admitted to myself this was actually going to happen and allowed myself to let time continue without scrutinizing every second that passed, wondering if I was dreaming or awake.

My metaphorical journey was metamorphosing into an actual physical voyage in just five short days. There wasn't a minute left to breathe if I was going to get everything done in time.

Chapter 15

Twenty-Four Hours on a Plane

———

FEBRUARY 2001

The physical journey to Vietnam was just as long and tedious as the paperwork journey. I left Chicago at 4:00 p.m. Sunday and would not arrive in Hanoi until 8:00 a.m. Tuesday.

As I boarded the plane from Chicago to San Francisco on Sunday afternoon, I felt as if I was making my first trip as a mother. Armed with multiple printouts of the tiny photo in my purse and more baby supplies than I had ever before seen stuffed in my checked luggage, I had no idea what this next chapter of my life would be like, but I couldn't wait for it to begin.

I had spent the previous week making lists, gathering supplies, organizing bags within bags and folders within folders when I wasn't on the phone and even sometimes when I was. The list of things I needed to pack "just in case" was vast, and I was mentally revising it nonstop.

Once I settled into my seat for the first flight of my adventure, I realized I had not thought of bringing any asthma medication. Although I hadn't really needed it in years, I didn't know what kinds of allergens might exist in Vietnam or what prescription options might be available if I needed them. I found a payphone in the terminal as soon as the plane landed and called Marc. I don't know how we managed it, but we both remained very calm as we discussed this clearly terrifying realization.

Marc efficiently used the internet to find a San Francisco Walgreen's close to the airport, where he called and urged them to prepare my inhaler as soon as possible. Meanwhile, I figured out how to find a cab and get myself to Walgreen's to retrieve the medication with plenty of time to get through customs and catch my next flight. I even managed to do this without yelling at anyone, crying, or in general freaking out to nearly the extent I would have expected. Maybe we could manage this parenting thing, after all.

The coach seat on my international flight was closer to my expectations for a first-class version, and I managed to pass the seventeen hours without incident. I was lucky to have an empty seat next to me in addition to all the comforts the enormous plane had to offer. I watched several movies on the personal TV screen built into the seat in front of me, ate several meals—they had both American and Asian choices— read a couple of chapters in my paperback, and even managed to sleep for a few hours.

I was the queen of compartmentalizing, and I had truly shown my skill on this flight. If I had allowed my mind to wander, I would have probably had a panic attack. Not only was there the forty-hour journey that I couldn't even wrap my head around but the thousands of unknown details awaiting me upon arrival. Somehow, I managed to focus on *When Harry Met Sally* and the lovely tea sandwiches being served, totally ignoring the enormous metaphorical mountain I was climbing by just sitting in that plane seat.

When I arrived in Hong Kong, it was very early Tuesday morning. How did that happen? Time zones are a mysterious thing. None of the multitude of interesting-looking shops were open yet. I had several hours to kill, so I wandered the hallways window-shopping. I sauntered along, making note of any place I really wanted to go into when we stopped for the layover on my return trip.

Eventually, I found a coffee shop that was open and had computer terminals available for reading and sending email. I was thrilled to send an update to Marc and the friends and family on my email list that I had arrived in the Far East and make the announcement that my excursion was officially underway and seemingly on track so far.

I also checked in with Marc on the phone. He said the agency called him but they just said they would be in touch with me when I arrived at the hotel. This didn't sound alarming or concerning, so I didn't think much of it. After hanging up with Marc, I was bored but couldn't really focus on my book, so I just sat and watched as the airport slowly came to life for the morning.

Finally, it was time to get on the plane for the final flight separating me and my child. The Vietnam Air plane was tiny, outdated, and cramped, especially compared to my previous chariot. The Asian food they offered me smelled terrible, especially so early in the morning.

I barely noticed these details, though. The flight was a mere two hours, the same time it takes to get from Chicago to Philadelphia. When we had gone to Philly or New York a multitude of times throughout my life, it had always seemed like a substantial flight. But now, after the San Francisco to Hong Kong leg, the 120-minute jaunt, give or take, was barely enough time to even think about what I would do in the following days. I never even removed my book or bag from under the seat in front of me. I just sat and let my mind race without allowing it to stop and worry over any particular detail.

As I stared, mesmerized, out the window over Vietnam, I was able to see land for the last forty-five minutes of the flight. I couldn't stop myself from weeping as I watched the endless rice patties and huts appear in the countryside as we got close enough to make out the details. I kept thinking, *This is the country that is giving me my daughter.* I couldn't take my eyes off of it.

I don't know what the middle-aged Asian man seated next to me was thinking, but he was clearly uncomfortable and sorry for his seat assignment as he watched the tears flow uncontrollably from my eyes. I didn't care. I was overwhelmed with emotion, and it was one of my truly happiest times, possibly of my entire life. I felt at peace, comfortable, and sure everything was as it should be. I was flying somewhere over my daughter, and I would be bringing her home very soon. I had managed to survive the endless flight I had been dreading in a mature, confident fashion. I must really be a mom. This was what I had been longing for since that day at the barn more than two years before.

Despite my lack of sleep, when we landed in Hanoi, I practically skipped down the aisle of the cramped plane. This was my destiny. I was practically jumping out of my skin. I was so ready to drink in all that this magical land had to offer.

Chapter 16

Where's the Facilitator?

FEBRUARY 2001

Once again, the road I was traveling and expecting to be concrete and smooth as glass turned to a rocky path overgrown with weeds in the blink of an eye.

The incredible, surreal, joyful excitement I felt on the plane lasted about an hour and a half in total. It started sometime during my flight to Hanoi, and the magic continued for just a short while after we landed. We walked down a portable staircase to the tarmac, where we boarded a bus that seemed to have been driven straight from a movie set of the Vietnam War. There was no glass on the windows or doors, just open spaces with fringe hanging from the roof as the cool air blew over us while the loud engine drowned out any other noise. Even as we arrived in the tiny crowded airport, I felt veiled by the mysterious quiet mood that had taken over my mind.

I remembered my previous concern when I saw the very rigid men in uniform who would interrogate and approve the passengers through customs. This mild unrest in my mind was short-lived as my assigned soldier smiled widely and congratulated me when I told him I was there to adopt a baby. He didn't ask another question before stamping my passport and directing me to the baggage claim area on the other side of glass doors.

The swarm of bodies filling the area on the other side of the door was loud and directionless. After retrieving my duffels, I had to struggle to lead my enormous pile of luggage through the crowd to the airport exit. Just then I realized I didn't really know who or what I was looking for or headed to. I had been told just that the facilitator would pick me up at the airport. I guess I didn't think to ask for a name or description of "the facilitator" before I left the US.

Eventually I found a bus driver from the hotel holding a sign with my name on it. I was slightly confused that this was clearly not "the facilitator," but the cloud of euphoria that had begun on the flight was still keeping me from getting too concerned or upset. I loaded my mountain of luggage and allowed myself to mindlessly gape at every aspect of my surroundings as the old van carried me to the hotel.

I checked in and made it to my room without incident. I tipped the man who brought up my luggage, looked around the room to get my bearings, and breathed a sigh of relief as I sat on a comfortable bed in a cheery, clean, and pretty room.

I then realized it was about eleven Tuesday morning, I was in Hanoi, Vietnam, and I was alone. The bubble burst rather suddenly at that moment when I allowed it to sink in that since the facilitator was supposed to pick me up at the airport, I had not even requested a phone number or way to get in touch with her. The two women who were supposed to be my travel companions were nowhere in sight either. I tried to find my previous serene attitude as I took the elevator back down to the lobby, but the edges of my patience had begun to fray.

I asked at the front desk where my fellow travelers were and was informed that they had gone shopping and would be back to meet me for lunch.

Okay, I could do this. I had made it here. Hadn't I? I was not going to let myself freak out, so I closed my eyes, shook my head clear, and asked where I could find a payphone.

I had gotten specific instructions from my long-distance company at home about how to call the US from Hanoi. I was armed with a local number, an 800 number, and a code to type in to any payphone in the country of Vietnam. Supposedly, this would allow me to then dial my home number and be connected to the United States. Unfortunately, none of these numbers got any response from the rusty receiver I was holding as I stood on the street corner near my hotel. No matter how many times I tried the number, the only answer was a solid dial tone on the other end of the line. No problem. I would just move to plan B, or was it plan C or D?

The nice young man at the front desk smiled as I again approached and inquired where I might find the computer with internet connection I was assured would be available at all times. He kindly directed me behind the desk and gave me a card listing office hours and rates. The secretary happily relinquished her desk and chair to me as she sauntered outside for a cigarette. Apparently there was only one computer for the entire hotel to share. *I'm not in Kansas anymore!* I reminded myself to breathe as I listened to the chirpy song coming from the computer as the modem dialed up a connection and slowly offered me access to my only tie to reality.

I had an email from Marc that sounded concerning.

Jen,

the agency called trying to reach you. They asked if you had gotten to Hanoi yet. I don't know why they wouldn't know this since they made your flight reservations. Have you met up with the facilitator? The agency said there's something wrong with Viet. The lab tests from her physical just came back last night, and she's not healthy. I don't know all the details but I'm sure you are getting more information from the facilitator. Please email me and tell me what you are finding out on your end. Love, Marc

This did not sound good! The next email came from the agency.

Mrs. Asher,

I'm sure you have already spoken with the facilitator regarding Viet's test results and the other available babies. Please let us know when you have made a decision about which one you would like.

I didn't read any further before hitting the reply button and responding all in caps.

WHAT FACILITATOR?? YOU SENT ME TO THIS ALIEN COUNTRY BY MYSELF AND NO ONE IS HERE!! NO FACILITATOR, NO TRAVEL COMPANIONS, NO ONE! I AM HERE ALONE AT THE HOTEL AND HAVE NO IDEA WHAT TO DO.

YOU NEED TO GET THIS FACILITATOR TO COME HERE NOW. SEND ME HER PHONE NUMBER. AND EMAIL. AND NAME!

*I JUST SAT ON A PLANE FOR TWO DAYS TO END UP IN A
HOTEL ALONE SO I CAN GET A SICK BABY THAT I CAN'T EVEN
BRING HOME!*

And then I realized it was just past midnight in Virginia
and my email would clearly not be received or responded to
any time soon. I hit send anyway. They should feel my pain,
even if it wouldn't be for another nine hours.

The cloud of serenity was really dissipating now. I was in
a full-blown panic.

Just then I heard activity in the lobby. My fellow future-
moms had returned. I logged off the computer and joined
them with open arms and a worried face. There were three
women. Jan, who I felt I already knew, was a tall woman with
short dark hair and wire-rimmed glasses. I recognized her
voice immediately and her face somehow matched the warm
Southern drawl. Jan was standing with a heavy woman from
Iowa named Pat, who was traveling with her friendly and
sweet-looking mom, Cindy.

They told me they were also concerned about everything
going on. They had met with the facilitator the previous day,
who had asked them to tell me she would be at the hotel
tonight to meet with me but had failed to specify a time. They
confirmed and clarified the news I had gotten by email that
both Viet and Jan's baby had tested positive for Hepatitis B.

None of us were familiar with the ramifications of this
diagnosis, but it seemed clear from what the women were
told on Monday that these babies were simply no longer an
option. The facilitator had tried to convince the women that
this was no big deal because other babies were available.

I returned to the computer and did a bit of research. I
learned Hepatitis B is common in Asian countries but

extremely dangerous for children. When babies or children have the disease, there is no cure. It eventually causes liver cancer. It also can easily be transmitted through bodily fluids in the same way as HIV. If we were to adopt a child with this condition, we would literally be required to wear gloves even to change every diaper and the baby would not be welcome at most daycares or preschools. This was clearly not a disease Marc and I were prepared to manage.

All three women were obviously concerned, and they also felt they hadn't been given all of the information yet. They hoped and expected to learn more tonight now that I had arrived.

Other details had worried Jan, too, she confided when we were alone. When they were taken to the embassy to have their paperwork stamped, the facilitator didn't go in with them. The woman at the embassy did approve the paperwork. However, she also took the two prospective mommies into a room back behind the desk, closed the door, and gave them a list of things that should concern them about their agency and facilitator, who was also *my* agency and facilitator.

The other Americans in the embassy waiting room, who were working with a different agency, were not taken into such a room. They also seemed to have their facilitators with them in the embassy.

For some reason, Jan had also felt as if they were being watched all the time and was convinced their room was bugged, although they had no proof. She said the front desk workers at the hotel always seemed to know where they were going or would give the women information before they even asked for it. Our agency had recommended this small hotel, and now we believed the connection went a lot deeper.

Everything the women had been told by the facilitator was very vague. All three American women were not comfortable but trying to go along as they were supposed to.

I would do my best to put an end to that, I thought. I was not going to let things go on that shouldn't be happening. As soon as I got to meet this facilitator face-to-face, I would set things straight and get the real story.

For the time being, however, there was not much I could do. No one would be coming to meet with us for at least seven or eight hours. So, in my typical fashion, I asked where the girls had been shopping and demanded they take me there. Shopping is one of my favorite hobbies! We stopped up at the rooms where they displayed their purchases and then headed right back downstairs and into the street.

We hired two rickshaws because they were the fastest transportation and negotiated a reasonable price in dong, the currency of Vietnam (I think it was about a dollar, but I wasn't positive), for them to take us to the market area. I tried to put the facilitator out of my mind as we were pedaled down the narrow streets, making small purchases along the way. Every walking street vendor we passed was a cousin of one of the drivers, and the more we rejected their wares, the cheaper they got. By the time the conical hats were priced at a dollar for four (one for each of us), we realized we had overpaid for our fare.

The market was so busy and exciting I managed to be fully distracted by the fast pace and great bargains. I couldn't believe the beautiful wares for sale and how inexpensive they became if we didn't agree to the initial prices. As an American who rarely travels, I am truly amazed whenever I visit a foreign country at how little relationship there is between the price marked on an item and how much the vendor expects to actually sell it for.

We looked at intricately embroidered tablecloths, placemats, and napkins. We saw hand-carved wooden instruments, bowls, and boxes that had been sanded and polished until they were as smooth as glass. We ooed and ahhed over tiny Au Dais in vibrant colors made of soft, delicate silk. We purchased a few small items and made mental notes about many others we wanted to come back for. Before we noticed any time had passed, we saw that the sun was starting to set and realized that we should head back to the hotel.

As our drivers, who had also followed us around the entire market carrying our purchases (we really paid too much for the fare), whisked us back to the hotel, reality began to sink in again. I remembered why I was there and what I would have to deal with when the facilitator arrived at the hotel to meet us. I lost my appetite and decided I would wait for dinner. I didn't want to take a chance we might miss our meeting by going out to eat. Jan agreed, and we all decided to gather in my hotel room and organize our thoughts as we waited.

We would present a united front. We all wanted some answers and clarification about why these babies were sick and why we were told to come over here before this information had been obtained. We wanted to know what was going on at the embassy and if this facilitator was going to be able to help us adopt children we would be able to get through the INS and bring home. We wanted to learn what was going to happen in the next few days and if all of the paperwork would be done properly.

The other women were quite taken aback by my direct manner and willingness to actually ask these types of questions. I was surprised they hadn't already gotten answers themselves and had allowed this craziness to continue for days.

This entire situation was completely unacceptable. One way or another, I was going to find out what the deal was!

Chapter 17

Baby Shopping

FEBRUARY 2001

We hoped things would clear up after the facilitator arrived, but after her visit we had just as many questions and concerns as we did before she got there.

As we compared notes about the agency and the other women gave me a full report of their time already spent in Vietnam, we heard a knock on the door. The room went silent as we realized that the facilitator had finally arrived. Jan jumped up to answer the door as I shut my eyes and tried to remain calm and collected.

I'm not sure what I expected "the facilitator" to look like, but it was definitely not the tiny young woman who now stood in my hotel room. Did I say woman? That might be a bit of a stretch. If I had to guess in normal circumstances, I would have said she was likely a high school student of maybe fifteen or sixteen. She was followed by another girl who I would have placed as a year or two younger still and who didn't open her mouth once.

I knew these girls must be at least in their twenties, but they both had beautiful long silky black hair pulled back in pony tails, and they were wearing neat but very casual jeans and blouses, which only added to their youthful appearance. They were also so petite, standing right about five feet, and the two of them together likely weighed less than any one of the American women in the room.

As the young women whisked in, they had huge grins on their faces and the "older" one gathered me up in a bear hug that caught me completely off guard. She gushed in broken English, "I so happy you are here safely!" She further explained, "We had orphanage meeting today. So sorry we can't come to airport for you." My previous anger turned to bewilderment at this strange encounter.

I sat quietly but became a bit dizzy as they went on with the sing-song report of their day and retrieved a pile of papers from their briefcases.

The older facilitator introduced herself as Julie—the first time we actually got a name for her—and her assistant, Mindy, who only smiled and handed her the papers she had been carrying. Then they both sat down on the hotel bed in front of me and the other women settled around us, in the single chair, on the floor, and on the extra bed in my room. Julie continued in her melodic voice to explain about the babies without taking a breath.

"So sad, baby Viet have the Hepatitis B. So many babies now have and can't get families," she said in her broken but understandable English. "Don't worry, ma'am. Other babies you can take. Her papers are right here. You look! You like baby Minh? Baby Ping? Look at papers. See pictures," she urged me to go through the paperwork.

I couldn't really wrap my head around this. I had been walking around with the photo of baby Viet in my purse, taking it out to admire the beautiful features at every stoplight.

I had shown that photo to everyone I saw since I got it in an email more than a week ago. I had memorized the tiny face and felt like I already loved her. How could I just switch babies without a second thought?

"I don't understand," I protested. "The agency told me Viet had already been to the clinic in Hanoi and was healthy. I don't want to switch babies. There must be a mistake."

But my question was ignored. "You like baby?" Julie prodded me while pushing the paperwork with a photo of a different tiny face paper-clipped at the top into my hands. "We change baby name on papers when you choose."

I could see now why Jan and Pat hadn't gotten any answers for the last two days, and I was determined not to allow this to be brushed under the rug. "Please, tell me why I came here for Viet if she was sick. Her name is on all of my paperwork. She already had a checkup at the clinic last week, and she was fine."

Julie sighed and cheerfully tried to get past this point, "Sometimes it take longer for blood tests. Doctor thought Viet was good but then blood came back. Baby Minh and Ping have good blood. Look at pictures. So cute!" It seemed this was the best answer I was going to get. "Paperwork no problem. We cross out Viet and put baby Minh name on them," Julie assured me.

From what I could understand, if I liked the paperwork for one of the two "new" available babies, Julie was claiming that we could just put her name on my dossier and get it approved at the embassy tomorrow. Then we would travel up to Lang Son to see the babies at their orphanage on Friday. If I didn't like the papers for the new baby "Minh" she was showing me, I could look at the papers for baby Ping. Ping had been premature but was doing well now. Baby Minh definitely appeared robust and healthy in the photo, but she wanted me to be clear that it was my choice.

I tried to look over the papers for the "new" baby girl Minh while Julie continued to relay further information. My mind was swimming with all of the details that had just been thrown at me in a single breath. I wasn't sure these were the details I was looking for, and I had a million questions if I could manage to put my thoughts into words.

I had to sort through the information she had just given me before I could formulate an inquiry or comment. Her English was pretty good but not great. I lost some of what she said from the language barrier. Beyond that, it was just a lot to take in all at once.

All of my great plans of being strong and getting to the bottom of the situation seemed to have either flown out the window or somehow gotten lost in my massive luggage, which was still not unpacked. While I listened to the facilitator go on with more details about what would happen this week, I waded through both packets of paperwork.

I think I just nodded with a glazed look on my face as I heard the rest of the plan. The assistant—the younger girl who told us to call her Mindy, which was clearly not her name—would pick me up from the hotel at eight the following morning so we could be at the embassy when they opened at nine. Julie—I was pretty sure also not her name—would double-check on the medical records for the baby I chose, along with Jan's baby, but would see us later in the day tomorrow. Beyond that, I didn't hear anything more she said.

Julie asked if I had any questions, but I don't think I could gather myself enough to actually make my mouth move before they were gone again. I was left in my room with the packets of paperwork about all three baby girls—Viet, Minh, and Ping. I was supposed to decide which one I was most comfortable with that evening so we could write that baby's name on my paperwork before we left the following morning. The other women went to the restaurant for dinner, but I didn't feel hungry. I was too distracted, so I told them to go without me. I also hadn't slept in more hours than I could count, so I stayed behind to sort out my thoughts.

After a few minutes of going over and over the papers, I went downstairs and sent Marc an email asking him to call me at the hotel. It was next to impossible to make a call to the US, I had learned. The pay phones were not set up for international calling, and all of the operators only spoke Vietnamese. I could call using the hotel phone and operator, for the small fee of about seven dollars per minute, but it usually took several tries before it actually got through, and then it sounded like I was talking into a tunnel with a loud echo.

Marc had told me to send him an email when I was at the hotel, and he would call me from home. He was literally on the computer 100 percent of the time except when he was sleeping or in the bathroom, so he would get the email virtually instantly. This was not easy for him either. I couldn't imagine being on the other end of the earth with such limited information.

I returned back to my room and waited for the phone to ring. I shuffled through the papers again, but my eyes were beginning to blur. I ate an energy bar, which I was really glad I had brought with me. I hadn't actually eaten anything since the flight from San Francisco to Hong Kong. Maybe I could lose a little weight on this trip? Eating didn't seem to be a big priority.

When Marc's call came through about ten minutes later, he told me it wasn't much easier to call Vietnam than it was for me to make calls. He had tried six or seven times, but the line always dropped before it was actually connected. Fortunately, we had set it up before I left with an international calling plan, so it was only seventy-two cents to call me from home, a 90 percent savings over the hotel rate!

I summarized the day's events for Marc and told him about the paperwork I had been staring at. We agreed it didn't make any sense to even consider any of them but the one baby who appeared to actually be healthy. It was nice to know there were options, but we had to go with the recommendations we were being given.

"Good luck," he said sincerely.

"I wish you were here," I told him, and I wished it more than I could say.

I barely hung up the phone before dropping off to sleep. Tomorrow would be a huge day.

Chapter 18

Different Baby

FEBRUARY 2001

There was no way for me to prepare for the day ahead. It was like being in a crazy spy movie, and I just had to keep my wits about me to get through it.

I slept fitfully, despite my extreme exhaustion. I had fallen asleep around ten but then awoke several times before my wakeup call jarred me to life at six o'clock in the morning. I was startled and leaped out of bed, ready to get moving. I still felt slightly weary, but I was somehow energized for the day to come. I showered quickly and dressed in a comfortable but nice-looking pantsuit for my visit to the embassy. I dried my hair and got downstairs before seven.

As I got off the elevator in the lobby, I realized I was quite hungry, which was not a surprise given the minimal snacks I had eaten in the past two days. The hotel rate included breakfast, so I followed the fragrances to the restaurant down the hall. I had expected to see a choice of cereals and pastries, with maybe some fruit, as you would find in an American hotel where you were paying fifty-nine dollars a night. Instead, I was greeted by a cheerful room with crisp, white tablecloths, delicate fine china, and sparkling crystal.

The perimeter of the room was lined with tables piled high with food.

One side of the room had tables sporting an American breakfast. I was overwhelmed with joy as I took in the most beautiful breakfast spread I had ever seen. A tower of bagels was surrounded by lox, chopped egg, tomatoes, cucumber, onions, capers, and an array of flavored cheeses. This single display was enough for me to praise this as an extraordinary breakfast, but it was just the beginning. Next to the lox tower sat another mountain of food, but this one was constructed of a rainbow of fresh-cut fruit. This display continued to include a tower of pastries, one of smoked fish, and heated platters of bacon, biscuits, pancakes, waffles, and French toast.

Around the corner from the gorgeous breakfast I recognized was a table just as big that was prepared for the Asian guests and one that must have been a traditional breakfast for Europeans.

The first was lined with aromatic heated trays, each with its own little candle beneath it. There were no less than a dozen Vietnamese dishes, none of which I could identify. Some had noodles, some rice; others had varying combinations of meats and vegetables. The third wall was a bit intimidating to me. It had piles of sausages and meats that might be used for sandwiches, and a chef stood carving ham, turkey, and roast.

I didn't go any closer to the meats and sausages; it was early in the morning, and my stomach couldn't handle that type of food just yet. I headed straight to the final area, where I found a variety of juices and teas that looked friendly and appealing.

I poured myself a glass of a melon-colored juice, which smelled amazing, and sat down at a table. Before I could put down my purse, a waiter was behind me, unfolding my napkin and placing it on my lap. He asked if I would like coffee or hot tea, or if he could get me anything from the kitchen. I couldn't believe there was anything the kitchen could make that I didn't already see, but he said, "Of course! What kind of eggs would you like?" I passed on the eggs but gratefully accepted the dainty porcelain cup of hot tea before heading back to the bountiful offerings surrounding me.

I loaded a plate with bagel, cheese, fish, and a sampling of every variation of fruit available. I also placed a tiny spoonful of two of the Asian specialties that looked relatively safe and vegetarian in a small separate bowl. I had been warned that meat in Vietnam could be dog or cat, so I should be sure to get descriptions if I didn't want to taste Fido for breakfast. I ate every drop of my selections and felt great! If this was what I had to look forward to in the next week, it might actually be fun. This country certainly had good shopping; now I knew the food was amazing as well.

The lovely waiter brought me a Styrofoam cup with fresh tea for the road and I gave him my room number and a tip before heading out to the lobby right on schedule. The front of the hotel was filled with exquisite furniture upholstered in silk. I sat happily on a comfortable sofa facing the main doors and watched CNN on the TV in the corner until my ride arrived.

The facilitator's assistant, Mindy, eventually came through the front entrance. She was about twenty minutes late but unapologetic. She asked if I was ready to go, and we popped out the door and into a waiting taxi. She asked which baby I had chosen after looking through my options. When I told her, she smiled and said, "Good choice!" (Why did I feel like I was buying a used car?) She pulled an envelope out of her bag that contained my dossier and proceeded to cross out Viet's name wherever it had been written and replaced it with Minh. She assured me this was legal and shouldn't be a problem. "Happens all the time," she explained confidently. I don't know if I was completely convinced, but I was satisfied enough to drop the subject.

The cab stopped at a corner, and my guide signaled for him to let us out. She paid him and ushered me to the sidewalk. We sat down at a small table in front of a café where she gave me directions.

I was to cross the street and go about a half block further down. The embassy was a large white building, and I couldn't miss it. I should go in, take a number, show them my dossier, and sign wherever they asked me to. Further, she instructed me, I should not mention I was working with a facilitator in Vietnam.

The US INS had been investigating more of the cases where facilitators were involved, so I should only give them the name of the agency in the US. If I was asked who was helping me here, I should just tell them "a representative from the agency." I was not very comfortable with this. I wanted her to come with me. I didn't like feeling as if I was hiding information or doing something wrong.

I started to voice my fears, but Mindy quickly brushed them off. "We're not doing anything wrong," she assured me. "They have just started looking at things closer, so it is easier to play their game than to answer lots more questions." She saw the skeptical look on my face and giggled. "You be fine. Your friends were fine Monday, and I do this with families every week. You don't need me. They like when Americans strong and go by themselves." She was playing on my ego. I took a deep breath and reminded myself that I had gotten all the way to Vietnam alone.

"I wait for you right here," she quipped before ducking inside the café. Suddenly I was on my own.

This just didn't seem right. My thoughts traveled back to the comments Jan and Pat made the day before about their visit to the embassy. I was trying to stay calm. "Trust the process," I kept telling myself. I had been told before coming to Vietnam that people here, especially women, were not so forceful as I was used to back home. I was trying so hard not to argue and question everything I was being told.

I gathered my purse and envelope before confidently heading down the street. I took a deep breath as I climbed the stairs to the embassy. Then, as I passed through the front door of the white building, I immediately felt as if I was in an office back at home. While I was still on edge, the feeling was more like being sent to the principal's office than to Mars, which was how I felt at the café with Mindy.

The staff was friendly and Caucasian, and the furnishings looked typically American. I took a number and sat down on one of the many available chairs as the handful of other people waiting watched me.

My number was called in only a few minutes, and I happily approached the window. The woman asked me a few questions to complete the top form of my packet, which had not been filled out yet. Included in these questions was the one I had been warned of. What were the names of my agency and facilitator? I answered as instructed, and the middle-aged woman on the other side of the glass grimaced but didn't comment.

The woman started going through the forms, checking each one off of a list she had. Several pages into the pile, she came across one of the forms where Viet's name had a line through it and was replaced with Minh. The woman did a double-take. "What is this?" she asked curtly.

"Oh, we had to change babies," I explained. "Viet tested positive for Hepatitis B after I had already left the states and the forms had been filled out. Minh is healthy, so we are taking her instead." I was back to feeling like I was buying a used car.

The woman shook her head and looked at me as if I were a child. "You can't just do that," she tutted.

I told her my agency said I could.

"No," she scoffed. "They should know better than that." She gathered the papers back into a pile and handed them through the dish under the glass that separated us. I didn't take them.

"You'll need to fill out all new paperwork with the correct baby's name."

"But I can't," I wailed. "My husband is back at home!"

"You could have him send it," the lady offered.

I tried to explain FedEx took at least four days from the States, and I was planning to leave in only four days! But the lady didn't hear me. She had already moved on to the next person.

I grabbed my purse and paperwork before storming out of the building. Mindy would just have to come back with me to take care of this. Obviously, there was some miscommunication.

I made my way back down the street and crossed at the corner. Suddenly, I realized there were several cafés on this street, not just one. I didn't know how I could have missed them earlier, but now I wasn't sure which one we had been sitting at.

I closed my eyes and tried to breathe. *I can figure this out.* I scanned all of the tables on the sidewalk but saw no young girls who looked familiar. I ducked into one of the tiny shops that seemed like it might be the place. I could quickly see only one elderly woman was tending the claustrophobic hut and ducked back out before she could ask me any Vietnamese questions I couldn't answer.

Breathe, I reminded myself yet again. I had a card for the hotel. I could give it to a cab driver if I needed to find my own way back, and I had money with me. There was no reason to panic.

I stepped through the next door I came to and exhaled with relief when Mindy jumped up from her seat close to the floor and came rushing toward me. "That was fast!" She delighted in her heavy accent.

"Yes, that is because they wouldn't approve me!" The words came pouring out. "They said it is *not* all right to change the baby's name. They said I would have to get all new paperwork from the United States. I am not staying here that long. Do you know how long it took me to do all of this paperwork? How are we going to fix this?" I was ranting, and clearly this woman with limited English skills couldn't take in everything I was saying.

"You didn't get the papers stamped?" She looked both confused and concerned. "It not okay to change baby's names?"

Mindy pulled out her cell phone and began speaking noises into it that I can only assume was really fast Vietnamese. The sounds I heard seemed to be even faster and more frantic than my English. For several minutes she talked nonstop, barely pausing to hear what the person on the other end had to say. Abruptly she snapped the phone shut. With as much confidence as she could muster, she told me, "I take you back to the hotel, and Julie will come handle it this afternoon."

This was not even close to being okay for me. "How exactly will she handle it?" I wanted to know. It was now only 9:30 in the morning. "Why will she not deal with this until this afternoon?" I was only here for a very short few days, and our schedule was tight already. We didn't have half a day to throw away when this was clearly a dire situation.

The girl seemed to shrink into herself, and I didn't know if she didn't know how to answer the questions or if she didn't even understand the questions themselves. "Julie not at the office right now," was basically the only response that I received. "She won't come back until the afternoon." Mindy was doing her best to stay collected and professional.

"No!" This was simply not an acceptable answer.

"She has meeting." She was clearly making this up.

Still not enough. "Well, when will the meeting be over?"

This went back and forth for a few minutes without making any progress. "Call her back," I demanded, pointing at the cell phone. She didn't want to, but she could see I wasn't budging.

After a shorter version of the frantic Vietnamese babble, the phone went back in her pocket, and she told me Julie would cut her meeting short and be back in the office by noon to start working on how to handle this.

I'd had enough. Since my arrival the previous day—how could that have been only twenty-four hours ago?—NOTHING was as it should have been. Every assurance I had gotten from the agency now rang false. The facilitator was not at the airport. The other ladies weren't at the hotel. The message to meet the facilitator didn't include a time or location. They had sent me to Vietnam without being sure the baby was healthy. Mindy sent me in to the embassy alone. They didn't know ahead of time it was not okay to change the babies' names. That was a lot for one day.

I was not leaving anything more up to chance. I was only supposed to be in Vietnam for a few days, and I had no time to waste. Mindy was with me now, and I wasn't letting her out of my sight until I had some answers. I obviously couldn't trust these people and was no longer willing to leave details for them to arrange without sharing with me.

"Fine." I stood up and moved closer to her. "I'll wait for her at the office. Take me there."

"No, no!" she cried. "You can't come to office. We call you when we know more. You wait at hotel."

"No." I was putting my foot down. I would not go back to the hotel until I had some answers. I was going to wait at this office until we had a plan and they explained how they were going to get me a baby.

This time the phone came out much quicker and the banter sounded desperate. After several pleas to the other party, Mindy handed me the phone.

Julie on the other end was slightly calmer than her assistant, but I would still put her in the "flustered" category. "I will be back to the office at noon, and I will get this taken care of." I could tell she was doing her best to keep her voice even.

"No problem," I replied. "I will wait for you at your office."

"No," the calmness was diminishing by the second. "You can wait at the hotel. I will call you there."

I took the same strong stance I had moments earlier and repeated the same basic argument until the women who were clearly taught to show immense respect could no longer evade the situation. Exasperated, she finally said she would meet us back at the office and asked to speak to her assistant. I smiled as I handed Mindy the phone.

I heard no more frenetic babble, just an occasional "yes," along with a nodding head. As the phone snapped shut a final time, Mindy made an almost imperceptible motion for me to follow as she turned wordlessly to walk out the door.

I don't know what I expected the office to look like, but it was definitely not the room I would shortly enter.

Chapter 19

Lifting the Curtain

———

FEBRUARY 2001

Clients had literally never been allowed to see this "office" before, and shortly I would understand why.

I sat in silence for what seemed like an extremely long cab ride. It could have been only a few minutes, or it may have been the better part of an hour. I had no concept of time, and all of the streets looked eerily similar.

I sat alone in the back of the taxi while Mindy took the front seat, directing the driver. Just yesterday this young girl was a complete stranger. Today she held my fate in her hands. I was expected to trust her to manage the most important transaction of my life, and she was clearly just a child herself.

I also had to trust she was actually taking me to the office and not to some place where I would conveniently disappear, never to be seen by my family again. After all, I was virtually alone in a very communist country where I didn't speak a word of the language and didn't know a single other person. I made a conscious decision not to allow my thoughts to travel in this direction.

I just had to believe everything was going to be fine. I would call the agency once we arrived at the office, where they must have a working phone, and they would find a way around this snag. The calm and pleasant voice back in Virginia, who prepared me for this trip, would know someone at the embassy to call and clear everything up. We could return the following morning and get all of the paperwork squared away. I could then use this incident as leverage for them to help me as quickly and efficiently as possible in the future. Yeah, right.

The mood in the cab was tense. I was angry and scared. Mindy clearly was off her game and dealing in uncharted territory as she told me several times clients were not allowed in the office. Even the driver seemed nervous, like we were headed into an area of Hanoi where an American woman should not be going.

When the taxi finally came to a stop, the neighborhood did not look like it would house an office. We were on a quiet, run-down street that seemed mostly residential but somewhat deserted. My thoughts returned to the subterranean tunnels left over from the Vietnam—or here, the American—War. I had the feeling a little Jewish girl's body could easily be irretrievably hidden. Well, I had no choice now but to have some trust in this girl, follow her, and keep my mouth shut.

My body wanted to stay in the cab as Mindy exited, hand the hotel card from my pocket over to the driver, and get the heck out of this place. But instead I forced myself to open the door and follow Mindy.

We filed down the dim hallways of what appeared to be a very cheap and outdated hotel. It felt eerie and musty, like regular cleaning was not included in the room rate. Mindy unlocked a tattered door with an old-fashioned key.

As we stepped inside the cramped room, I saw a very barebones tiny hotel room, dingy with basic furniture stuffed into it that was very old and worn. The small desk, filled with two computers, a printer, and fax machine, looked out of place.

Mindy told me yet again how this was highly unusual. No other American family had ever been allowed to see the office before. I could tell she was extremely nervous, and I could understand why. My confidence I would ever actually see a baby was diminishing quickly.

The air in the room felt stale and had a negative energy. It was dreary, depressing, and would be considered a slum back home. I tried to calm myself by investigating the room while I listened to Mindy's incomprehensible and frantic phone conversations that continued, one after another. This was clearly over her pay grade, and she was trying her best to hold herself together.

I literally prayed that Julie would get there quickly. After looking around, I sat on the office chair positioned in front of the desk and wondered if I could use the laptop computer to check my email. I would ask Mindy, if there was ever a pause between phone calls, but it seemed unlikely she would be taking a break any time soon.

Julie swooped into the room after we had been there for about fifteen minutes. She also had a cell phone attached to her ear and finished her call before saying hello.

She forced a smile as she asked me for details of my meeting at the embassy. As I relayed the story, she nodded but cut me short.

She had been on the phone with my agency lady, she reported, and had good news. The agency had forged a relationship with a new orphanage in Thai Nguyen, the one-trip province where I was originally supposed to go. Six baby girls were actually available there, but they had not yet been to the health clinic.

This was good news, for sure, but just sounded so *shady*! They all of a sudden had a new orphanage in the province I had been told a week ago had no prospects coming up? There just happened to be not one, but *six* baby girls available? Why would they have babies that hadn't been to a doctor? None of this seemed right, and I opened my mouth to protest and ask these questions, but I snapped it shut before any sound came out.

After all, I was in a tiny dingy hotel room somewhere in Vietnam with two total strangers. What really were my options here? The best I could do was trust them and quietly pray everything would work out.

"I have a meeting all day tomorrow," Julie sighed, "but Mindy take you tomorrow afternoon to Thai Nguyen to see babies." Oh, no, I was being stuck again with this nervous young girl who clearly didn't know what was going on.

"If you see baby you like at Thai Nguyen, we bring babies to clinic in Hanoi for physicals Monday," she went on. "Then you go home, do paperwork, and send back, because it one trip Province. Friday, we can all go to Lang Son, where Viet and Minh are," she continued. "Just in case."

I was scheduled to fly home Saturday, and it was now Wednesday. Why would we wait a full day to go to the orphanage when we had so little time? I could no longer trust these women to make good decisions on my behalf. I was going to need to take charge if I didn't want to be stuck in Vietnam indefinitely.

"No," I told her with as much calm and kindness as I could muster. I was done being compliant. "Why can't we go see the babies in Thai Nguyen today?" I asked. "It's early still." I didn't want to sit around Hanoi for the rest of today and tomorrow morning. I was in this country for a purpose, and I wanted to get everything resolved as soon as possible.

Julie looked exasperated and worn down, but she could see there was no arguing with me. With a great sigh, she picked up the cell phone and resumed her string of calls. Mindy did the same. After several conversations, of which I obviously couldn't understand a single word, both girls eventually snapped the phones shut and compared notes.

Mindy would escort me back to the hotel where I was instructed to gather my gifts for the orphanage along with the things I would bring up for the child I chose. Julie arranged for a van to come collect us from the hotel in just over an hour. It would be a long drive up to the orphanage, so I should eat something before we left. I had won!

My head was spinning from everything I had orchestrated in the past hour. I'm not sure exactly how I managed this and silently thanked my father for teaching me smart negotiation skills.

I was still trying to clear my head when the cab deposited me back at the hotel, and I was relieved to see the three American women sitting in the lobby. They all wanted to know everything that happened, and I tried to quickly recap the crazy morning I just lived through.

They queried me about my trip to the embassy and were all shocked and surprised that I had gone back to the facilitator's office. I asked them to come with me up to my room so I could gather my things as I gave them a full report.

I was desperate for the women to accompany me on the trek up to the orphanage. However, both Jan and Pat had already planned to go with Mindy to actually formally submit their paperwork at the embassy. After much negotiation,

Cindy, Pat's mom, agreed to come with me. I was so grateful! This was a big deal.

On the surface, the drive would be over three hours long, and Julie's English wasn't likely to hold up to a conversation longer than a few minutes. More importantly, meeting these babies for the first time would be emotional. I didn't know what kind of conditions to expect in an orphanage.

Besides, I was still very skeptical about this whole situation. I had concerns about these facilitators and about the agency itself. Nothing was going as planned, and a lot of details seemed to be hiding behind a wall of smoke and mirrors. I wanted to be able to take mental notes about the trip, the orphanage, and about Julie herself. It would be really helpful to have another set of eyes confirm what I was seeing. After the morning I just experienced, I didn't think my brain alone could file everything away accurately if the afternoon proved to be as full of intrigue and bizarre details as the morning had been.

It was truly a gift to have Cindy join me. I knew she would rather be with her own daughter and present when the paperwork for her granddaughter would be submitted. It was kind of her and Pat both to make the decision for Cindy to come with me.

The three women went down to have a quick lunch before we went our separate ways. I took the time to pack one of my duffel bags for the orphanage. I was still pretty full from breakfast and much too excited to eat. I was going to meet my baby for the very first time!

Chapter 20

The Orphanage

FEBRUARY 2001

My "journey" took on a whole new meaning when I traveled to the rural province deep in the countryside of Northern Vietnam.

As we settled ourselves in the van for our excursion, I was extremely grateful for my own foresight. Without the substitute mother who was accompanying me, I don't think the afternoon would have been bearable.

First of all, Julie rode in the front seat and conversed in Vietnamese nonstop, alternating conversations between the driver and her cell phone. My companion, Cindy, and I exchanged glances and raised eyebrows several times as the travel moved quickly from the highways of Hanoi to narrow paved roads and, before we knew it, onto even narrower, unpaved dirt "streets" that looked more like paths.

We cringed each time a car was coming from the opposite direction as it skimmed by us, only inches from the side windows of the van. We drove through an area that was seemingly endless rice fields with workers in conical hats scattered among the greens. The "towns" we went through were no more than clusters of grass huts in a small clearing between the fields. I felt as if we were traveling backward in time.

As we got further into the more rural areas, Julie continued chattering away, and we figured out her string of phone calls included several that were giving her ongoing directions about how to get where we were going. As the scenery became more foreign and farther from the bustling city streets of Hanoi, I found myself increasingly surprised and appreciative she still had a cell phone signal.

The van was very stuffy and didn't have air conditioning. Although the climate in Vietnam can be scorching, it was February, and since Hanoi is in the north end of the country, it felt like crisp fall days while we were there. Although the temperatures had been relatively cool, probably in the seventies, and we were heading even further north where it should be even cooler, the sun was beating down through the windows. It raised the temperature in the van higher than was comfortable. We couldn't have the windows open at all because the road was so dusty it would be impossible to breathe if we did.

After about an hour and a half on the road, Cindy and I were beginning to really sweat, and Julie told us that we were going to stop for a "Coke." While we were relieved to get a drink, we were concerned when we saw where it was coming from. The "store" was basically a mat set out in front of a hut with a barrel of ice and some pitchers. Julie hopped out of the van and returned with two glasses of brown liquid for her and the driver and two unopened sodas in cans like we had never seen before.

We were scrutinizing the cans we held but were not so distracted that we didn't notice a young girl who slyly slid in beside Julie quickly before the van zoomed off. I tried to quietly and covertly catch Cindy's expression out of the corner of my eye. She seemed just as bewildered by this woman's appearance as I was and was trying just as hard to hide her expression.

We tried to busy ourselves so we wouldn't be staring at the mysterious new passenger. My companion and I looked at each other and then at the cans, considering our options. We finally decided if we wiped the cans really well with our shirts (no napkins were provided), they would probably be safe to drink since they were sealed shut. We shared one of the warm but sweet, fruity sodas, saving the second for later. After coming to a decision on the refreshments, we could no longer distract ourselves from the elephant in the front seat.

We whispered almost silently, trying to guess why we had acquired an additional passenger. However, we knew they were watching us, and we didn't want to appear too concerned. Through our muffled whispers we decided at best this woman was just to help direct us how get to the orphanage, and at worst, she would be selling us into white slavery.

Unfortunately, we guessed the most likely answer was she was involved in brokering baby sales. To this day I suspect that was the case, but I have no proof, no name, no location, or even a mental picture of the woman in question. The whole day was so odd and such a whirlwind, there were simply too many details and too many faces for me to remember them all clearly.

After about forty-five minutes, the van again slowed, but this time absolutely nothing was in sight. We saw no huts, no makeshift "stores," no other people, just miles of rice patties. Again Cindy and I exchanged worried glances, just as our extra traveler hopped out of the van.

Before we could blink, she had disappeared over a hill, and we were speeding off in the other direction. To say we were confused would be an understatement.

We traveled on, and the road somehow managed to narrow even further; the dirt turned to gravel, so the van bumped along uncomfortably. It had become so bouncy it distracted us from the mysterious woman who had left so suddenly, and we became unsure if we had simply imagined her.

Just when we knew we couldn't get into any more foreign a place, a metal archway welcoming us to a large building appeared on the left side of the van. We knew this must be the orphanage because about two dozen children of varying ages were standing outside, awaiting our arrival. Cindy and I caught our breath as we realized the significance of this site. These were all orphaned children. They were beautiful, and somehow, my daughter was among them.

We sat in the van while Julie got out and met with the withered old man who ran the operation. We were hot and tired, and tears ran down our faces as the children all gathered around, peering in the windows. Some were shy and held back while others came right up and knocked on the glass. We had been given strict instructions not to leave the van, and at least I was grateful. Although I was literally itching to jump out and see the babies, I knew I needed a moment to compose myself and mentally adjust to the scene. It was beyond overwhelming, and I felt unsure how we were going to interact with these foreign youngsters who would obviously speak a different language.

We got out of the van when Julie returned with the wisp of a man that she motioned for us to shake hands with. Then he passed us off to a little old woman—possibly his wife—who whisked us away, saying she would bring us to the babies. As we followed her, behind us was a train of children, all curious but silent.

She led us into a tiny room about one-fourth the size of my hotel room. It had only one small window and the open doorway, so the room was dim and stuffy. As we entered, on the left were four bamboo cradles, all lined up on the wall. In each cradle was a tiny baby, wrapped from head to toe in layers and layers of blankets. Only the beautiful little faces were visible, and they were all sleeping in their little cocoons. Past the cradles was a single rocker and a door that led to a small bathroom. On the right wall was a small bed with two other baby pods asleep side by side. We were quickly steered away from those two and told they were the twins, who had already been promised to a family and needed to be adopted together.

The room was crowded. Not only were my companion and I followed by a string of at least six children, but there were also three young teenagers who were the babies' caretakers, busy making bottles and folding blankets. I tried to take in the scene as I gazed at the precious dolls in the cradles.

At first I was afraid to pick them up, but the caretakers encouraged us to unwrap them, hold them, feed them, and examine them. As I looked in each bundle, I stopped when I got to the third cradle. The tiny eyes were open, and they looked at me as if they knew me. I couldn't help but scoop up the child and cradle her in my arms. She was exquisite. I had never seen a face so beautiful. I felt as if I were falling in love at first sight, and I couldn't take my eyes off of her.

Cindy had a great time holding each of the other babies, feeding them bottles and changing the rags (they don't have diapers) inside of their blankets. It was clear she would be a great grandma, and she was relishing the opportunity to get some hands-on practice with these tiny angels.

I tried to make a show of playing with the other babies as well, but I didn't want to put the precious gem I had discovered back in her cradle.

We took lots of pictures despite the lack of light, and before we knew it, Julie was telling us it was time to go. She had already taken care of handing off the monster-sized duffle bag of clothing I brought for the orphanage, and she instructed us to say good-bye to the children.

We had talked to the teenaged babysitters and learned a little about the infants. All of the babies were about three to seven weeks old. We learned their names, and they were all doing well.

We also met a wonderful young girl, aged six, who had a much older girl behind her, almost being carried piggyback. The babysitters told us the older girl was blind, but her best friend carried her around all the time, and they could never be seen apart. They both loved the babies, so they spent a lot of time in the nursery where we had been. It was a heart-warming, tender sight, and I felt my eyes fill with tears to think of the love between the two girls.

All the children got along and played perfectly. They were clearly their own family and loved each other immensely. It was so touching and wonderful. Despite the lack of food, clothing, toys, family, literally everything, these children were happy and playful. Tears streamed down my face as we pulled out of the drive, watching the children wave and even run after the van.

The picture of all the children, especially the beautiful baby I struggled to let go of, was burned into my mind. I was so excited to get the actual photos developed and to write an email describing the incredible images to Marc. My heart was full as we headed south toward Hanoi and we sat in silence, letting all we had seen sink in.

Chapter 21

Night Life

———

FEBRUARY 2001

I was bursting with joy after seeing the orphanage in Thai Nguyen. Everything was finally back on track! The perfect baby I imagined for so many months was now real, and I knew in my heart she would be mine.

When we returned to the hotel in Hanoi, Julie laid out the plan for our next few days.

None of the babies we had seen in the orphanage had been to the clinic yet. The caretakers would leave very early the next morning to bring all of them down to the clinic in Hanoi. They could all be examined so I would know before leaving the country if the baby I had chosen was healthy. If she was not, I could "pick" from the other available babies.

They were coming down early so they could be the first ones seen when the clinic opened in the morning. It would be a very long trip for the caretakers and babies. The facilitator would pick me up at 7:30 a.m. so I could meet the babies when they arrived.

I was beyond ecstatic and couldn't wait to tell Jan and Pat about our day. I gave them a full report about how bizarre the ride and orphanage were and how beautiful "my" baby was.

Jan and Pat had already had dinner, but poor Cindy was starving. I was once again too excited to eat. The three of them headed down to the hotel restaurant, and I decided to go for a walk to get my photos developed.

I asked at the hotel front desk where I could go and got directions. The photo "shop" was just a few blocks away, but he said I shouldn't really go out alone at night. I should wait until the morning. I thanked him for the information but ignored his advice. I couldn't possibly wait any longer to see the beautiful face of that baby again.

So I walked in the direction I had been shown and slowly entered a whole new world for the second time that day. It was the true Hanoi in all its glory. The hustle and bustle were like you'd expect to see in any large city during the height of the business day, but it wasn't the height of the business day. It was about 8:00 p.m., and the sky was pitch black.

Traffic was crazy. Motorcycles, taxis, and rickshaws honked their horns pretty much nonstop in every direction I looked. The shops were all still open, and local cooks, craftsmen, and shopkeepers of all kinds were peddling their wares on every available inch of the sidewalk. I weaved through them as I followed the numbers I found on some of the buildings until I saw the little "shop" with the familiar Kodak logo behind the counter.

The shops all had open fronts with counters that faced out onto the street. I walked down the sidewalk and stopped at the appropriate counter. The woman at the photo place spoke no English at all and neither did any of the neighboring shopkeepers. I held out my rolls of film (this was before the days of digital cameras) and she understood I needed to get prints made. I tried to pantomime some questions about how much it would cost and then what time it would be ready.

She had absolutely no idea what I was asking. Finally I pointed to the clock behind her and she looked puzzled. A man sitting behind her knew enough English to say, "Tomorrow."

I shook my head as I said, "No," and pointed to my watch. "Tonight?" I asked with hope in my voice.

It was now eight and I guess they were planning to close in an hour. They finally agreed to have them ready at 8:45 by pointing at where the hands on the clock would be at that time. She tapped on her wrist where a watch would be to make it clear I should not be late, as they would be closing. I nodded my head vigorously, promising to be back at just that time. I gave up trying to get an idea of the cost. What did it matter?

I kept walking in the same direction as before, thinking of all the shopping and people-watching I could do in forty-five minutes while my photos developed. I rationalized if I just kept walking in the same direction, I couldn't get lost.

I was about a mile away from the hotel, but it may as well have been a hundred miles as different as the atmosphere was. The area where the hotel was located was clearly set up for tourists. The shops all resembled stores I would expect to see in the US. The streets were all immaculate with trees, plants, and grass carefully placed and maintained to create a beautiful environment.

Now I was in the real city of Hanoi. I saw no grass, trees, bushes, or plants anywhere. Small gatherings of people lingered every few feet, and everything looked dirty. I was on such a high from the orphanage visit that the scene delighted me. I was a world traveler! I was walking the streets like any Vietnamese woman would. I was completely oblivious to the fact that I stuck out like a sore thumb. I was twice as wide as even the largest people I passed and taller than most of them. (At five-foot-three and a size ten, this was not the position I was used to being in.)

I was also the only person not talking. Most of the people were either talking in a group of people, commenting to their friends as they passed, or chatting on a cell phone. It was incredibly loud, especially to my ears because it all just sounded like gobbledygook. None of the noises even sounded remotely familiar. Because Vietnamese is a tonal language, the sounds are extremely different from English. But none of this bothered me.

I flitted from shop to shop. Some of them were closing up, but many were still open. I inspected what some of them were selling, but little of it held any interest to me. Some simple clothing was for sale along with some extremely cheap Western-style children's things, but most of what I saw was pantry-type items. These were not the items meant for tourists that were sold during the day.

Cans of unusual-looking soup, sauces, meats and vegetables were stacked on shelves or on the ground. Interspersed between the endless cans were some boxes of noodles, crackers, and such, and cellophane-wrapped dried items that appeared to be fish, vegetables, fruits, and possibly meat. Some of the items I could identify as carrots or octopus, but most could have been just about anything. I wasn't quite sure what I was looking at most of the time, and of course all of the labels were in Vietnamese characters. Occasionally one of them would have a picture on the label that would give me a clue.

I did buy some chocolate candy that had a photo of berries next to the odd characters describing it. The berries looked good, so I thought I would give it a try.

Although most of the shops were getting ready to close for the night, the "restaurants" were just getting started. Little fires were built right next to the sidewalk with pots above them of bubbling broth. Clusters of men and women sat on the ground or at little tables sipping broth or popping unidentifiable morsels into their mouths without the slightest pause in their conversations.

The smells were overpowering but pleasant. Some were delicious and familiar, but most were unusual and very interesting. I was walking on air and fortunately not hungry at all, because I had not done much research about what types of things were safe to eat.

I had been checking my watch, but time was moving very slowly. It was 8:25, and all of the shops and restaurants were beginning to look exactly the same. I would walk just a little more before heading back to find the photo shop again.

Just then, I was walking along, minding my own business, when a young Vietnamese boy appeared out of nowhere about two feet in front of my Nikes. Before I even knew what had happened, he laid a live chicken on the sidewalk with one hand, and the other hand, holding a knife, swiftly swooped down from the air to remove its head. I stopped dead in my tracks, but the boy didn't even see me as the blood ran down the dirt. I turned on my heels and knew it was time to head back.

My saunter in one direction was replaced by a purposeful march in the other. The bubble I had been floating in was bursting a little from the sight of that chicken, but I was so excited to see the photos I still felt like a kid in a candy store. This was my baby's homeland, and no beheaded poultry was going to ruin that for me.

I again followed the numbers, making my way back to the address written on the hotel card in my pocket. It was about 8:50 when I arrived at the right number, and I could tell the woman had been watching the clock, not sure I would return at the appointed hour.

She wrote down the price for me, about twenty dollars for double copies of the three rolls, and I paid them in dong as I flipped through all of the prints.

The tiny and perfect face appeared among the photos of the market and rice patties, and I had to smile. It was just a matter of time before this would be my daughter. I was starting to truly believe it.

I power-walked back to the hotel and was slightly sweaty and breathless when I arrived. My traveling companions were waiting for me in the hotel lobby. They couldn't believe I had been wandering the streets of the city by myself for the past hour and a half.

I quickly showed off the photos but wanted to head right back out to find an internet café. I had to send these pictures off to Marc so he could get his first glimpse of our future child! Jan volunteered to go with me because she wanted to send some emails as well, and the computer at the hotel was painfully slow. The helpful man at the front desk told us there would be a better connection at the café.

This time we hailed a cab and handed the driver our hotel card with the address written on the back. The internet café was in the same neighborhood as the hotel but too far to walk. It was right along the immaculate center square in town across from a beautifully kept park where people seemed to do yoga or tai chi at any hour of the day.

We went in, found terminals, and got an employee to help us scan the photos in to the computer. I was able to email a few of them to Marc and tell him the details of my day. The connection was a lot faster than at the hotel but still incredibly sluggish compared to what we were used to at home.

Marc and I emailed back and forth a few times since he was waiting at the computer to hear from me, especially after I had called him earlier in the day to relay to him the incredible story of my morning. How could this possibly still be Wednesday? It was about 10:00 p.m., and I was completely exhausted.

Marc was encouraging but skeptical. He agreed that the baby was cute, but he couldn't see her as ours yet. Too much would still need to fall into place before that could be real to him. I didn't let this deter me and insisted he forward the photos to our friends and family. By the time we finished at the café and caught a cab back to the hotel, it was very late.

My eyes were already closed as I collapsed on the bed in my room, but the phone rang almost as soon as I lay down. Marc's voice greeted me and instantly made me feel comfortable and like myself again.

The reports I sent via email were too incredible to believe, and he wanted to hear them straight from my mouth. I went over again what would happen the next day, and we discussed the concerns we both had. Before he hung up, he agreed to call over to the agency and have them call me back to confirm I was understanding everything properly.

I fell into a deep sleep as the clock said 12:30, and I knew I had to get up about six.

The ringing phone jolted me awake and I sat bolt upright less than two hours later. The agency lady had gotten Marc's message but just got time to call me back. I was a little annoyed with being woken up at 2:00 a.m., but she was encouraging and happy I was so pleased with the baby at the orphanage.

She said they didn't even have the paperwork on these children yet, but I should be confident Julie and Mindy knew what they were doing. This was not quite what I wanted to hear, after viewing that day just how "professional" the facilitator and her office were in person. She assured me it would all work out and she was excited for me to go to the clinic the next morning. She would check in with me again the following evening (morning her time) to see how it all went. I was able to drift back to sleep in a relative peace, happier than I had been in a very long time.

Although I would get only a few hours of rest, I was actually eager for my wakeup call, because it would mean I was about to see my beautiful baby again.

Chapter 22

♪ Always Be My Baby ♩

FEBRUARY 2001

The bliss of the past few hours would be short-lived. Before I saw my baby again, yet another surprise phone call would redirect my course again and shatter my newfound happiness.

My wakeup call came at six, and I leaped out of bed and into the shower. I dressed quickly and realized I hadn't had anything to eat since the previous morning.

I returned to the beautiful breakfast downstairs, which fortunately opened quite early. I filled my plate with a piece of French toast, bacon, and some fruit. When I returned to my table, however, the waiter was there waiting to tell me I had a phone call. I glanced at my watch, but it was too early. Julie shouldn't be there for another half hour.

When I reached the house phone, it was the voice of the agency lady who had previously been so calming to me on the other end. "I don't know how to tell you this," she stammered, "but the baby you saw yesterday has been assigned to another family."

I did not take this news well at all. How could that possibly have happened? I was here, in a strange country, where this agency had sent me by myself. I had done everything as I was supposed to, yet everything had gone wrong. They only had an arrangement with the orphanage for a day or so. How could they have assigned my baby to another family?

She said she understood my frustration and they would try to get the referrals switched. For right now, though, I should go with the babies to the clinic anyway. One of the other babies I had seen was still available, so I should go and see what the doctor had to say about her.

I didn't want that baby. They told me I could have the darling baby I now viewed only as my own. They couldn't take her away from me now! Let the other family have the available baby. They weren't here to hold her as I had, see her little face in person, and fall in love with her the way I already had.

The agency lady said she would do her best, but it was already evening in Virginia, so nothing could even be looked at until the morning. She had been waiting at the office well past closing so it would be late enough to call me in Hanoi. She gave me instructions to go to the clinic, and she would talk to me that evening when she returned back to the office for the morning in Virginia.

Well, so much for eating. I felt like I might throw up, and I didn't have time to eat now anyway. The wonderful waiter had seen what was happening and already put my tea into a Styrofoam cup. He offered to pack up my food as well, even though it was a buffet, but I didn't think I would be able to eat it. I took my tea and moped down to the lobby. I stopped in the office and dashed off a quick email to Marc, letting him know about the latest turn for the worse. I didn't want to hear from him that he told me so. I just wanted to make it through the morning without crying. Fat chance of that.

I was already holding back tears when Julie walked through the front door, asking if I was ready to go. When I looked at her, the tears started streaming down my face. She said, "Okay, I guess you heard about the baby you liked yesterday. Don't worry. Other baby is yours now."

"No," I told her, "the agency will get the referrals switched. I just talked to them."

She said she didn't know about that, but the other baby was very cute and I should go for her exam now. I was angry but didn't see much point in arguing. I just followed her to the waiting cab and felt very alone in the back seat.

When we got to the clinic, the babies were already there. There were five in total, including the twins, and each one had her own caretaker to carry her. They also each had some sort of dirt on their foreheads. One of the nurses explained this was to give them good luck for a safe journey down to Hanoi. The babies were brought in to be examined one at a time.

They wouldn't let me go in with the baby I wanted, despite my loud protests that things would be switched and she was going to be mine. They said if that happened, I could talk to the doctor on the phone at that time. I was outraged but felt defeated.

They said this was someone else's baby, and I didn't have a right to her medical information. I grudgingly accompanied the baby who had now been assigned to me into to the examining room. I tried to listen as the doctor reported on her general health and gave me specific numbers like her temperature, height, and weight, but I couldn't bring myself to think of this as my own baby.

The doctor was European and spoke with an accent that was not Vietnamese at all. However, he sounded much more familiar to me than anyone I had spoken to recently. He was very nice and said he understood my frustration. He promised he would be more than happy to talk to me on the phone about the other baby later, but he had to follow the facilitator's instructions today.

The exams took much of the day, and it was mid-afternoon when I said goodbye to the babies, caregivers, and Julie. I took a cab back to the hotel by myself. My mood fluctuated between extreme sadness and outrage. It was a horrible feeling of helplessness. I felt like a fish out of water. I had been in this country for two full days now and I had barely eaten or slept.

I didn't like the feeling that nothing was quite kosher, and on top of that, it wasn't being done for my benefit! I was eager to talk with the agency again and make sure they got me the "right" baby. I knew I would have to wait several hours before I could do that and had to keep myself distracted.

I called the other girls' rooms when I got back to the hotel, and they hurried down to my room, wanting to hear about my visit to the clinic. They weren't expecting the news about the other baby assignment or my phone calls from the agency.

We decided to go down to the hotel restaurant for dinner, where I relayed the day's events and confided to the other girls how I was coming to distrust both the agency and the facilitators. None of what was happening was adding up. Telling me the baby had been given to another family was just the final straw.

Seeing the dismal hotel room "office" of the facilitators the previous day felt like pulling back the curtain in *The Wizard of Oz*. These people were not the professionals I had been assured they were. Reputable businesses who charged families thousands of dollars would not be running out of a tiny, cheap hotel room.

Other things had me suspicious as well. Jan and Pat told me themselves they thought the rooms were bugged and our emails were possibly being read. They told me again about the unusual "talking to" they received at the embassy before my arrival. Certainly I was concerned when Mindy didn't come into the embassy with me, particularly when I saw other families with their facilitators sitting next to them once I got inside.

These were all signals that something wasn't right. I felt as if my attention was being directed away from the whole situation, over and over again. I continued to dismiss these signs because I was so sure that baby was to be mine, but I couldn't get over the uneasy feelings.

The plans were changed so drastically, so quickly. Reputable professionals should have been able to foresee the problem at the embassy with changing the babies' names. This shouldn't have been such a surprise.

Then, out of the blue, another orphanage was available? Before I agreed to go on this trip, I was assured this alliance would not likely be forged any time in the near future. But then somehow, within just two days, a new orphanage was on board with the agency. So odd! And then within those two days the babies had been assigned to other families even though the agency and facilitators all knew we were here in Hanoi and visiting the babies in person?

Possibly the most bizarre twist was the mysterious woman who jumped on and off the van. None of us could come up with any logical explanation for that part, and we were all searching for a reasonable answer.

The three of us were trying so hard to trust these people and believe in their process and that they would be able to help us bring our children home. I wanted to believe it, too, but it was getting more difficult as these suspicious clues kept popping up.

Jan agreed with me but optimistically hoped for some logical explanation. Pat, on the other hand, didn't want to hear it. She just wanted to believe there was no problem here and wanted me to stop making trouble. She asked me to stop calling the agency and stop harassing the facilitators. She wanted to meet her baby and go home. She didn't want to hear any more of my theories and basically just wanted me to shut up.

I was very distracted by my thoughts. I knew things weren't right but managed to get through dinner. Again, the hotel restaurant meal was delicious, extravagant, and cheap, but I was so upset about the babies and worried about our entire situation, eating wasn't a priority.

Talking with Pat wasn't helping either. She didn't want to hear what I was saying. She wanted to go with the flow and not question anything going on. This attitude did nothing but annoy me, and it was a miracle we managed to keep our voices from raising high enough to alert the whole restaurant. I needed to get away from her to save my sanity.

I also wanted to get back to my room in case the agency was to call. I already ducked down to the office to email Marc three or four times, so he was totally updated on the little bit I knew. If he talked to the agency, he would make sure they called me immediately, and he would keep trying to call them until someone answered the phone.

When I got back to my room, I turned on the TV to CNN, the only channel in English. Before I had watched for ten minutes, I couldn't keep my eyes open any more. I drifted off to sleep for over an hour before the phone ringing dragged me up from the bed.

Marc called at about nine to say that he talked to someone at the agency and they would call me as soon as they knew something. I had so much emotion bottled up before I answered the phone, and now I couldn't stop sobbing. It was just too much for me.

Marc tried to calm me down. "It will all be okay. Being upset right now won't help anything." I kept him on the phone for a while, trying to adopt his attitude. He assured me he would be on top of the agency that day and we would get some answers.

I finally calmed down a little and let him get off the expensive call. I managed to get back to sleep, but it was a very troubled sleep. I kept waking up and looking at the clock. I wanted to talk to the agency! Why hadn't they called me yet? I thought about going downstairs to email Marc again, but I didn't have the energy to get out of bed.

Finally the phone rang sometime in the middle of the night. It startled me out of my sleep, and I wasn't the most pleasant when I answered. The lady at the agency told me she hoped to have more information before she called me. However, she still didn't really know anything. They wouldn't be able to find out more about the referrals until Monday.

This did not make me happy. She told me I should go with the other girls up to Lang Son later that morning. I could meet baby Viet in person and see baby Minh and Ping as backup plans in case they weren't able to get the referrals switched and I didn't want the baby I had gone to the clinic with that morning.

She had also talked to the other ladies and said she understood I had not been getting along with one of them. She recommended they set up a second cab for me to go in for the trip to Lang Son. The agency would pay for it because they felt so badly about everything that had happened.

I told her I did not want to go up alone. I thought the lady should just get over it and grow up. We could certainly all ride in a car together. Before we hung up, she agreed and said it was silly. We were all adults and could take the ride in one van.

Chapter 23

I'm Going Home

FEBRUARY 2001

I tried to face this day with courage and calm. I was determined to have a nice time on the trip and help take photos of all of the babies in yet another area of this exotic and mysterious country. I was not expecting the signs that had been popping up to hit me over the head with another message that I should not be here.

When I got up the next morning, I had overslept a little. After waking up so many times during the night, I was definitely not well-rested. I threw on some clothes and headed downstairs. I stopped at the restaurant to get just a cup of tea to go for the second day in a row. When I got to the lobby, the other three women were there waiting already. They were all silent, staring at CNN and looking nervous. We said perfunctory "good mornings" but little else.

When Julie arrived, both she and Mindy came into the hotel. They rounded us up and led us to a waiting van. The other three ladies boarded the van first, and I started climbing in behind them when Mindy literally grabbed my arm and pulled me to a cab I hadn't noticed before, sitting right behind the van. She was strong for such a tiny girl! The young woman physically dragged me by the arm and shoved me into the cab as I called to Jan. However, Julie had closed the van door quickly as soon as Mindy had me a few feet away from the van's bumper. Before I was even in the cab, the van had pulled away. I didn't quite know what happened.

I asked Mindy, who just said, "Agency called last night. We think two cars is better. You want to go in separate car."

I said, "No, I want to go with everyone else!" But she just ignored me.

She was already on her cell phone, making nonstop foreign sounds again.

I sat quietly for a while, stewing. I couldn't believe that yet again I was in the back seat of a car with no one who spoke English in the front. And I was stuck here for a four-and-a-half-hour trip! The more I pondered this situation, the more I decided, "How *dare* these people!" I started to cry and couldn't stop. I wasn't thinking straight, but I knew I didn't want Pat and Julie to be able to treat me this way.

I went over the discussion from yesterday in my head and conjectured this was Pat's request, and Julie was dutifully following orders. They weren't going to get away with it. I wasn't going to put up with this anymore.

I didn't need to go to Lang Son. I needed to go home to my husband. I needed to get back on my own turf in a country where I spoke the language. I was completely overwhelmed, partially due to lack of sleep and food. But the more I replayed everything that had happened since I got off the plane in Hanoi until the present moment, the more I was convinced something shady was definitely afoot.

The agency and facilitators knew I was onto them. I asked too many questions and *demanded* they do things properly and responsibly. I wasn't willing to just go with the flow and brush any suspicion under the rug.

Now it seemed clear to me they didn't want me sharing my views, information, and suspicions with Jan and Pat. They wanted compliant clients who wouldn't ask questions or make demands. They were using Pat's anger and insecurity as an excuse to separate us. I needed to get out of this whole situation. I gathered myself together and told Mindy, "Please stop the car. I'm going home now."

We were on a very large (for Vietnam), busy highway, but somehow I had decided I would be able to hail a cab on my own and get back to the hotel. Mindy looked at me with terror in her eyes and said, "You want to go back to hotel?"

"No, I'm going home now." We repeated this exchange several times but she still didn't understand. Finally I put my hand on the door handle and said I would jump if they wouldn't stop the car.

Mindy yelled, "No, no!" Then she quickly dialed Julie's number on the phone, and soon both vehicles pulled to the side of the road. The two Vietnamese women literally jumped out of the cars and switched places. Julie sat down in the back seat next to me and touched my arm gently as the car started moving again. "What's wrong?" she asked in a soothing voice, but I wasn't fooled.

I tried to control the tears enough to reply confidently, "I've had enough. I'm going home now."

"You can't go back to Hanoi yourself, and Mindy and I need to take other ladies to orphanage," she explained.

"No," I was somehow calm now. "I'm going home. Either take me home or I'll go by myself." I put my hand back on the door handle.

"Okay!" she exclaimed when she saw my hand move, and she instructed the drivers to turn around. Both vehicles made a U-turn and headed back to the city.

I refused to say another word on the hour drive back. Julie sat with a concerned look next to me, refusing to open her phone again for fear I would threaten to jump if she didn't continue to babysit me. But I made a decision that I would have nothing more to do with these people.

I would pack my bags and go to the airport. My flight for the following day was scheduled to leave at eleven, and I was betting the same flight would be running today. I don't know why I thought I could just get on any plane I wanted, but I had decided I would do just that.

When our mini caravan arrived back at the hotel, I still wouldn't talk to anyone in either car. Both Jan and Cindy got out and tried to ask what was wrong. I just couldn't explain right then. I would call Jan when we were both safely at home in the states. I got out and walked straight into the hotel lobby without looking back.

I stopped at the front desk long enough to tell the lady working there I would be checking out early and to please have a taxi to the airport ready for me in fifteen minutes. I threw everything I had brought and purchased into my bags without folding anything. I called Marc just long enough to tell him I was coming home, and when he started to ask questions, I told him I had to leave and I would call him when I could.

I then hauled my luggage to the elevator and walked through the lobby with my head held high. The two Vietnamese and three American women were still standing by the large glass front doors of the hotel, trying to figure out what to do. I paid the bill for my room in cash at the front desk and strutted out to the waiting airport shuttle without another word to the women who all stood and stared at me in disbelief.

I rode to the airport and tried not to think about anything. I was taking deep breaths, had gotten myself calm, and wanted to maintain my composure. If I started crying again, I didn't think I would be able to stop, and I would need to keep my wits about me to be able to get myself home. I stared out the window the whole time and admired the landscape. I still had a fondness for this land, but it certainly had been tainted by my experiences over the last few days.

When I got to the airport, I walked up to the ticket counter and handed over my ticket. The Asian man looked at the paper and told me that it was for tomorrow. I told him very simply, "I know, but I need to go today." I didn't explain. I didn't say the ticket had been issued wrong. I didn't make excuses or lie.

The man looked at my puffy, bloodshot eyes, which had been crying for the last day. He started to question me but didn't seem to have the language skills. "I need to get back to the states today," I repeated, and he seemed so surprised to have a woman so confident and forceful that he just printed out a boarding pass and handed it to me.

I was barely in time as I headed straight on to the plane. It was less than fifteen minutes from the time I walked into the airport to the time that I stepped onto the jet. It was a good thing, too, because the plane took off very shortly after I sat down.

The flight from Hanoi to Hong Kong was empty and uneventful. The seat next to me was vacant, and I sat silently, in almost a meditative state, for the entire two-hour flight. I breathed a sigh of relief as I deplaned. It was as if I had escaped an alternate universe and could finally let down my guard a little.

I had only about an hour in the Hong Kong airport before my connecting flight to LAX. I called Marc again but still didn't tell him much. I just said, "I'm in Hong Kong and I should be landing in LA in about eighteen hours. I'm safe and glad to be out of Vietnam. I will tell you more when I am home in the US. I just need to take one step at a time right now."

I looked at a couple of the store windows I had longed to go in just a few days before, but now I couldn't even focus enough to ask any prices.

As I sank into the comfortable seat for my international flight, I could feel myself release the tension I had been carrying for the entire time I had been in Vietnam. I ate the surprisingly good airline food served to me just after takeoff and then slept for most of the flight. I woke up in time to eat one more meal before we landed. I may have to fly internationally more often. They seem to come by with food every hour or so! I only had enough time awake to watch one movie on the whole seventeen-hour flight back.

When I got to LAX, I went through customs and found a United ticket counter. The woman didn't have the same attitude as the man had in Hanoi. She told me in no uncertain terms that my ticket was for the next day and there was no chance of me getting on a flight to Chicago until then.

I didn't even care. I went to a public phone and called my sister-in-law, Betsy, who happened to live in the area. She fortunately was just leaving work and said she could pick me up in no time. She was happy to have me spend the night at her house and hear of my adventures.

I was back in a country where I understood everyone when they talked to me and they understood me. There were no mud shacks, beheaded chickens, or endless rice patties. I was home.

Chapter 24

She Will Be Mine

FEBRUARY 2001

I was glad to be back in the US, but I felt like a shell of myself. My body was weak, and my mind was like mush. Visions, memories, impressions, feelings, ideas, suspicions, and theories were all spinning around in my head so fast I couldn't grab hold of any single thought long enough to make sense of it. I would need to allow it all to settle before I could put together enough words for a conversation. Once that happened, the fear, guilt, and grief I had been holding at bay would seep into my consciousness and take over. It was easier to walk through life for the weekend as a disembodied shadow, allowing everything time and space to come together within myself on its own.

I had an uneventful day in LA. I tried to heal my body by filling it with the food and sleep it had been deprived of for so many days. My mind was another story. So much had happened in the past seven days!

The only thing I really remember about my day in Los Angeles was the call I made to the agency while I waited for Betsy to pick me up at the airport. I was still in complete denial about the entire ordeal, which allowed me to remain completely calm and collected for this call. I did not address my sudden exit from Hanoi and simply asked about the status of the baby in Thai Nguyen who I believed was destined to be my daughter. The agency asked why I had left, but I diverted the question with insistence on them answering mine. They reciprocated the brushoff and told me they had nothing to report; they would know more on Monday.

I maintained my composure as I assured them I would be calling back first thing Monday morning, and I know they didn't doubt it for a second. I had the impression their attitude toward me had changed slightly, and they were taking me a little bit more seriously. It was about time!

I visited with my sister-in-law and gave her a very surface-level and perfunctory report about how I had spent the week. I was able to answer questions vaguely and distract her by displaying my souvenirs from the trip. I knew I didn't have the emotional energy to delve into a true account of the disturbing events circling my brain, and I wanted to sort them out myself with Marc before trying to describe them to anyone else. I put on a great facade, and we were able to have a short but pleasant visit before she deposited me back at the airport the next day.

I flew home to Chicago, and I don't know if I was ever so happy to see Marc as when he picked me up from the airport. I had survived a major ordeal and was somewhat of a different person than I had been a week before. I felt more confident and accomplished for all I had seen and done.

For now, I relished my comfortable surroundings. I collapsed in my bed with my loving husband and dogs surrounding me. I ordered dinner from my favorite sushi restaurant and giddily drank in the tapes of my favorite TV shows Marc had recorded while I was gone. I spent all of

Sunday appreciating my life and the familiarity of everything around me. I allowed myself this day to not think at all and just let all the thoughts and emotions slow down in my head without trying to catch or consider any of them.

By early Monday morning, however, I awoke remembering the ache in my heart and the longing for a baby. I looked at the clock, but despite the time difference it was still too early to call the agency. I distracted myself until shortly after 8:00 a.m. and dialed the number from memory.

The woman at the agency sounded tired and weary. She reported there had been some developments over the weekend. I steeled myself for the news that the other family had already filed some irreversible paperwork tying them to *my* baby and was prepared to argue. I was not prepared for what I heard, however.

The woman said, "We are immediately terminating all adoptions at any stage of the process in Northern Vietnam."

"What?" was all I could reply.

"The INS has intensified their investigations in Vietnam, and our agency has made the decision to transfer all families from that program to other countries," she continued.

"Huh?" I'm not often left speechless, but the past week still had my head swimming.

"We've been meeting all weekend, and the decision was made because we don't want to risk families not being able to return back to the US with their babies."

I was shocked to say the least! "So basically," I asked, "my whole trip last week and everything that happened there was just irrelevant?"

"Pretty much," was her immediate response.

"But what about my baby?" I asked without a thought. "What will happen to her?"

"She will most likely be adopted by a family from another country. This is a problem with the US INS. Nothing about the Vietnamese process has changed on their side. In fact, our facilitator also works with families from Canada and all over Europe, and those adoptions are moving forward without the additional paperwork requirements."

I was relieved to hear my baby wouldn't live out her life in the orphanage, but I couldn't comprehend much of what I was hearing. How could the whole awful trip have been just an exercise in futility? There must be a way around this. The woman told me all of the program fees we had paid could be rolled over in full to another country. The agency would absorb the cost of working with the Vietnamese facilitator and embassy. "Talk to Marc and decide which country you would like to be switched to. I recommend Kazakhstan or Cambodia."

I didn't want to go to a different country! I wanted my little Vietnamese baby, not just any baby, but the one I had held, fed, diapered, and even loved just a few precious days before. After I hung up the phone, I sat on my comfortable bed and cried once again.

I called Marc and told him about the news. He said he would start looking into the other programs the agency had to offer. He was back in project mode.

But I couldn't join him in that mode. I wasn't ready yet. I felt the need to mourn the loss of this baby with an intensity that surprised me. I felt more sadness than I had when learning of my miscarriages. With the miscarriages, I was definitely sad. I felt the death of the growing child inside me, but I was able to accept that my body knew something was wrong. I trusted those souls weren't physically able to keep growing. They were taken from me naturally.

But this loss was different. It was more real. This was an actual, real-live baby, and I had truly thought she would be mine. I didn't want to give her up. The vision of leaving her behind in the tiny room of that orphanage, wrapped in layers of rags, flooded my mind. I wanted to go back and scoop her up in my arms forever. Somehow government rules and paperwork were blocking my path to her, and it was impossible for me to understand.

After I stopped crying, I called my friend Micki, the woman in Utah, to tell her of my travels. She had been so nice and helpful, and maybe she could shed some light on what had happened to me. I trusted her and thought it would be cathartic to explain my adventure and my loss to someone who had been there and understood the process.

I told her all about the trip and how scary it all was as well as how suspicious and awkward the facilitator seemed. I told her about the strange office in the hotel room and trip up to Thai Nguyen. I described the worker at the embassy and the mysterious woman who momentarily joined us in the van.

She wanted every detail and listened carefully. Then she quietly told me, "I may be able to help."

I didn't understand. I didn't want to start this all over, I didn't want to go back to Vietnam for a different baby, and I had my money all tied up with the other agency. But I was willing to listen.

Micki told me that after everything I had been through, the other agency would likely refund my money to avoid a lawsuit. Beyond that, she knew the orphanage that I had been to. Her agency had worked with that very same orphanage for quite a while, and if the other agency had terminated all of their adoptions in Northern Vietnam, the baby I saw should be available to be matched to me through a different agency. We would have to be careful, but she thought she could make it happen.

I began to cry again, this time with relief and delight. Maybe the trip wasn't a waste after all. Maybe it really was a voyage to meet my destined child. I hadn't expected this possibility but now realized it was exactly what I needed to hear. I'm not sure any other option would have kept my overwhelming anger at bay at this particular point in my quest.

Micki told me they recently started doing all of their Vietnamese adoptions through a man who was an independent facilitator in Hanoi. She would speak with him that very day, and he could personally go up to the orphanage with the name and birthdate of my baby to check on her and have her assigned to me and Marc.

She was literally typing an email to him as we spoke. She recommended I leave my money with the other agency for the time being, just in case. She didn't think I would have any trouble getting it refunded if we could make this work, but she wanted to be sure the baby was still available and cleared for adoption before I put an end to that relationship.

A wave of relief poured over and through me. I had trusted Micki from the first time I talked to her. She was gentle and kind. I now know she also had exactly the connections I needed.

Over the next week, I talked and emailed with Micki several times a day. She was on top of the facilitator, and he would be traveling to Thai Nguyen several times a week to make sure this happened.

He'd found my baby and spoke with the skinny old man I met at the orphanage. He made sure the baby wouldn't be assigned to another family and began investigating the paperwork available on her. He would need to make sure everything was done properly, or else the INS would not approve a visa for the baby, which was what the other agency had been afraid of. Micki was my new superhero.

Everything was looking great with Micki, and the agency in Virginia seemed perfectly happy to put our funds and application on hold while we took some time to make a decision about what other country we would consider adopting from. I think they were just happy not to have to talk to me for a few days.

The next couple of weeks passed slowly, and the news from Micki seemed to trickle in without much actual new information. She kept telling me the facilitator was still investigating and trying to identify and confirm all of the required paperwork existed and was signed properly.

But Micki was also worried about me. She knew how much I had been through and wanted to take care of me. She set up an online group of families who were all waiting to adopt from Vietnam. Her clients could then talk and help each other wait through the comfort of email. She insisted I join the group and lean on the other families for support. It was great to have other women to email with who were all going through the same thing.

I asked Marc to please talk to the other agency and inform them we weren't ready to jump into another country yet. We would investigate all of the options, but we needed some time. The agency was perfectly happy with that answer and said they would wait to hear when we were ready.

Eventually I pulled myself together enough to call Jan. It was hard for me to revisit anything related to that trip, but none of it was Jan's fault. I was worried about her too. I knew she had come home from Vietnam to the same news that I had heard on Monday. I was glad I called because it made the memory of our trip seem more real and less scary. Somehow it helped me to settle my mind.

The agency had been recommending Jan and Pat go to Cambodia to adopt because the laws were friendly for single women. Neither one of them had made a decision yet, but Jan was leaning toward following their advice and going to Cambodia.

I was glad to hear she had a plan and was feeling pretty comfortable with the agency, even after all we had been through. I was happy for her. I would consider this path as an option if I had to, but I wasn't ready to go there yet. I needed to follow my heart.

Chapter 25

Dossiers of Many Countries

———

FEBRUARY–MAY 2001

The spring of 2001 was a complete blur. Despite working harder and faster than anyone thought possible, the baby I longed for seemed to keep slipping through my fingers. I fought the urge to fall into depression and grief, holding on to the hope I could plow through this and find the light at the end of the tunnel. I would never have guessed where that light was coming from.

I had gotten home from Vietnam at the end of February and begun working with Micki immediately. At first, I was very excited about this change. I trusted Micki and had wanted to work with her from the beginning. Plus, she was promising me the baby I had already fallen in love with. I looked forward to talking with her every day. But by the second week, the "new" information she had for me was coming even slower, and I was getting discouraged.

I loved the new community of friends I had formed from Micki's email list. We had each other to lean on emotionally, and I was so glad to have them and grateful to Micki for setting up the group. It was a lifeline, and having others in the same boat at such times was priceless. But we also used the group to compare notes, and we were all having similar doubts. I had to fight to try and draw strength from them rather than allowing them to pull down my mood.

In the next few weeks, the information dwindled even further and then turned from no news to bad news. The required paperwork simply wasn't there. The facilitator hadn't wanted to report in the previous weeks that he had been scouring through records but coming up empty. The bottom line was the documentation the US INS would require simply wasn't there. In fact, the facilitator alluded to the fact that he thought this may be just the kind of situation the INS was concerned about. The baby was most likely not brought to the orphanage in the required manner.

As it was explained to me, either the baby had been stolen and the mother had not signed off on her, the baby had been purchased and brought to the orphanage by some person other than the mother, or the mother had been convinced to leave the baby but had not signed to relinquish her. She may have believed she could come back and get her at a later time.

It was also possible the orphanage just hadn't collected all of the required documentation. After all, the additional documents were new. Only the US was requiring them, so it was quite possible this orphanage just didn't have everything in place for the additional paperwork at the time the babies were relinquished. We would never know for sure. Regardless of how she had gotten there, the US INS was not going to approve the adoption of this baby girl.

I know about all of this because I did a whole lot of research on the web. I belonged to a larger group online of families adopting from Vietnam in addition to the smaller group formed by Micki. It had hundreds of members, from all over the world. Discussions on there ranged in a huge variety of topics. Families discussed the agencies and facilitators they used, gave tips for packing and traveling in Vietnam, and made recommendations for life with a Vietnamese baby after they were home.

A lot of discussion during this time focused around the INS investigations in the US. People shared links to newspaper articles and lots of personal reports of odd interviews families had at the embassies or with the INS. The INS was very concerned about facilitators seeking out young babies and essentially buying them from their mothers for about a thousand dollars each.

The INS was becoming increasingly strict on the completion of all required paperwork for relinquishment. Presumably, some of the paperwork was incomplete simply because it was never required or enforced before, but some of it was definitely corruption.

Upon hearing all of the personal stories of families being detained in Vietnam, I was beginning to feel lucky for getting out of there as unscathed as I had.

I was heartsick about the news, truly devastated, but I had started to predict and expect it over the previous week or two. This was a dark time in my life as I now felt the loss of three babies—the two I had miscarried and the one in Vietnam.

Marc took me out to dinner the night we officially relinquished the baby in Thai Nguyen, and he tried to get me to look forward. He said, "It's okay to grieve, but if you still want to be a mom, you should let this baby go and look at the options we have." He had done some research on the programs the Virginia agency proposed and thought both the Cambodia and the Kazakhstan programs looked pretty feasible. We discussed the timeframes, travel requirements, and more, and we decided to pursue going to Kazakhstan.

I was so lucky to have Marc, but I was terribly depressed during this time. I had worked so hard to get that Vietnamese baby, and now she was gone. I grieved for her once when I got home from Vietnam, and now I had to grieve for her again to be able to move forward. Marc really helped me find perspective and kept my head above water. The undercurrent of loss was still there, but together we could hold each other up and stay afloat.

Marc had managed to get me to accept the grief and get back into project mode. When we got home that night, I printed out the forms from the agency and began to research everything I could find about Kazakhstan. It didn't look like a very fun place to visit, but I refused to allow this fact to deter my plans. I was once again a woman on a mission!

The country was extremely poor, and the diet was vastly different from ours. It looked like the people there existed mostly on different varieties of horse sausage. Not my cup of tea! I found a family who had posted a blog of their Kazakhstan adoption and had packed an industrial-sized jar of peanut butter to eat literally every day of their trip. This sounded to me like quite a reasonable plan, given the typical diet there.

The children from this region were certainly beautiful, though, and it looked like the adoption process would fit within our cost and travel guidelines.

The next morning I called the agency and had them fax over any additional forms I would need to complete a dossier for this country. I talked to them extensively about the process and how to get through it as quickly as possible. I spent the next few days completing the entire Kazakhstan dossier and doing various forms of research. I talked to several families who had traveled to this region of the world and checked out every book I could find at the library.

Since I was now experienced at putting together a dossier, I was able to complete all of the paperwork in mere days. Fortunately, when collecting documentation for our original Vietnamese dossier, I had the foresight to obtain many of our documents in multiple copies, "just in case," which made things a lot easier. Within the week, I had put the whole thing together, seals and all, and FedExed it to Virginia.

In between collecting paperwork, I learned even more about the country. I discovered both Asian and Caucasian children were available for adoption there. Because most of the families adopting were from the US, the demand for the Caucasian children was much greater than for Asian children, and the wait for them was minimal. I found this quite disheartening, but it did work in my favor. It should make the process for me quicker and easier than I had expected. I was starting to feel my heart fill again.

After sending off the dossier, I waited expectantly to hear from the agency with more details about what would happen next and when. I heard they had received my paperwork but needed to review all of it. They said all of the documentation was there, but they wanted to have the Kazakhstan facilitator go through my home study. I thought this should be a piece of cake and began mentally preparing to travel again.

The news I heard next hit me like a ton of bricks. After having reviewed our file, the facilitator had some concerns. She didn't like that our home study made reference to the fact I had been in therapy while I was in school. She said all adoptions need to be approved by the court, and the judge might not find us a "fit" family because of that reference.

I could literally feel my heart sink when I heard this. Not only was this another dead end, but this time it was literally my fault. I had been in therapy as part of my schooling, and I had mentioned it to the home study worker. Now this one piece of information I shared was the roadblock to a child in Kazakhstan.

They had other concerns as well, but those were minor compared to the reference to my counseling. Apparently participating in psychotherapy holds quite a stigma in Kazakhstan. The bottom line was, we could try if we wanted to, but there were no guarantees.

We could travel quite quickly, get the baby from the orphanage, wait up to two weeks to see a judge, and then go to court. The facilitator felt there was about a fifty-fifty chance of our adoption being approved.

If the judge didn't rule in our favor, however, we would have to come home without a baby again. I didn't want to put myself through that trauma again. We would have to travel all the way around the world a second time with the distinct possibility that we would just have to start all over when we got back. I wasn't willing to do it, and Marc was adamant that he would not travel twice.

So, we were now back to square one, yet again!

I couldn't believe it. I felt the rug was being pulled out from under my feet at every turn. I spent at least a day in bed just feeling sorry for myself and questioning everything.

But I didn't want to give up. I had started this project, and I was going to finish it. Sheer resolve got me out of that bed and back to the computer. At least I was getting the hang of things now. I had gathered paperwork for our home study and two dossiers already. How hard could it be to do another one?

I was not going to let this take any longer than it had to. I contacted the agency yet again and told them that we were not willing to take the risk of going to Kazakhstan, and we wanted the paperwork for Cambodia. They faxed everything over, and I got to work.

I decided, this time, I wasn't going to put all of my eggs in one basket. While working on my Cambodia dossier in the evenings, I spent my days on the phone. I called every adoption agency I could find.

I talked to one agency who told me about a great program for adopting from Russia. Russian adoptions could be very dangerous. Because of the culture there, it was considered socially acceptable to drink during pregnancy. A study done by the Boston-Murmansk Orphanage Research Team found that over half of children in Russian orphanages show signs of Fetal Alcohol Spectrum Disorder (Miller et al., 2006).

Although I was wary of adopting from Russia in general, the agency I spoke with assured me they had a special situation there. They had an American physician who literally lived at the orphanage. This doctor took care of pregnant mothers who didn't think they'd be able to parent and then cared for the babies as well. She was able to report the level of alcohol use during pregnancy and very extensive details regarding the health of the babies. I had never before heard an agency offer this much information and careful monitoring of birth mothers. I thought this sounded like a good program, so I got the paperwork for this dossier as well.

I found yet another agency who had a different kind of program with Vietnam. It was owned and run by an American couple who had adopted several times from Vietnam. They now did all of the work in the US as well as the facilitation in Vietnam themselves. They didn't rely on anyone else's honesty or responsibility. I thought this sounded like a hopeful possibility as well. I was able to have the Virginia agency send me back my Vietnam dossier, and this agency told me how to tweak it for their program.

I contacted Micki again and asked what she thought. Micki had become a close friend over the past few months. Despite the fact she was unable to facilitate the Vietnamese adoption for us, she had remained professional, honest, and downright loving through the whole process. I truly trusted her and her opinions regarding all things about adoption.

Micki recommended going to China. She said the wait was long, but it seemed to be getting a little quicker lately. Her agency would allow me to submit my dossier without putting any money down right away. I had her get me all the paperwork needed.

I now had four different dossier "projects" to distract me from my despair. I still had nightmares about my trip to Vietnam and the baby I felt I had abandoned there, but during the day I was definitely keeping myself busy. These projects gave me a reason to get up in the morning and hope that my baby was out there somewhere.

It took about two weeks to get everything together for the four dossiers. I had piles of paper, folders, and notebooks strewn around my bedroom and home office. I had given up my job, wrapping up my internship early, so this adoption quest had consumed my life.

I continued to make calls to find other options besides the four programs I was applying to. At night I scoured the internet, just like I had at the beginning of this journey. I followed up on every lead. I spoke with people at dozens of adoption agencies and law firms. I investigated the logistics of every international adoption program to find others I could apply to without a large initial financial investment.

I was still afraid of becoming attached to a domestic birth mother who might change her mind, but I thought it may be possible for situations to exist domestically after children were born. I talked to agencies with domestic programs, asking all of them if they ever dealt with babies who were already born.

They all told me the same thing—almost never. But that didn't stop me from continuing to ask. I left my number with anyone who would take it, just in case something were to come up. I told everyone I got on the phone with about my experiences of the past few months, my trip to Vietnam, and that I didn't want to become attached to another baby or birth mom if I wasn't going to be able to adopt the child.

This all-out assault of the adoption agencies around the country began in April. By May, I had submitted four dossiers to four different agencies for four different countries. Each one of them was complete and waiting. I made the decision not to make a decision. I would just see where a referral came from first.

Fortunately, little or no money was required to be submitted with these dossiers. All of the agencies I had chosen required the fees to be paid only after a referral was available, so when the first one called, I could make a final decision at that point.

Regarding the domestic agencies, that didn't seem to be a promising path. Every agency I spoke with seemed to match families to birth mothers who just found out they were pregnant and wouldn't be due for another six months or more. Further, they required a large financial deposit up front to be included in their bank of families.

The process for domestic adoption was much different than the international process. It involved committing to one agency, giving them a large nonrefundable deposit, and creating a very extensive and elaborate scrapbook with photos of the potential adoptive family and a beautifully written letter to the birth mom.

Then any potential birth mom would be presented with a pile of profiles—the exquisite scrapbooks—from several families meeting any criteria the birth mom specified. They could then choose one of those families, interview several families, and then choose one or request even more families if they weren't smitten by any of the options given.

Then once, if ever, we were the chosen one, we would spend several months bonding with the birth mom, supporting her financially, and becoming attached to both the mom and unborn baby. Once the baby was finally born, the birth mom had literally no obligation to place the child for adoption, no matter how much money, time, and emotions we had invested in her.

This seemed like an extremely long and painful process. It also really turned me off to think I would literally be competing with other families to be chosen.

My bottom line was I wanted a baby of my own quickly. This had become my biggest priority. As time went on, my restrictions and limitations became much more lax. I cared little about the race of the child, I was willing to travel for longer than I had originally been wanting to do, and I rarely even asked what the cost of the adoption would be. I just wanted to be done!

I had tried to resume a normal life by May. While my thoughts were dominated by the pending adoption possibilities, I refused to allow my actions to be. While I was daydreaming all the time of what my future child would be like, I did my best not to show the world around me I wasn't totally present.

I was back to my routine as much as possible, shopping, spending time with my friends, and riding my horse. On Thursday, May 24, I spent the afternoon at the barn. I rode my horse, gave him a bath, and took him for a walk out in the meadow to eat grass. It was a beautiful day, and I was relaxed. I had left my cell phone in the car, as I always did because it didn't get a signal in the barn.

When I leisurely got into my convertible and turned on the radio at 6:06 p.m., I picked up the cell to see if Marc had tried to phone. It lit up with a message that I had missed five calls from a number I didn't recognize. This couldn't be good. Or could it? I had no idea how the rest of that day would be etched in my memory and change my life.

Chapter 26

I'll Be There

MAY 24, 2001

As I pulled out of the barn parking lot, I pushed the button on my phone to call back the number of my missed calls. It seemed like a long time before the woman answered the phone. "Hi," I said into the phone. "I've missed several calls from this number but I don't know who I'm calling." My skepticism was soon to turn to overwhelming joy, relief, and sheer euphoria before I even got to the highway.

"Is this Jennifer?" the woman on the other end of the connection replied.

Since I didn't recognize the number, I wasn't willing to give away too much information, but I assured her that I was, in fact, Jennifer.

"Oh, I'm so glad you called back! I've stayed at the office late hoping you would."

She had my interest, but I still wasn't sure what this was about.

She began by asking me a bunch of questions. "Are you the woman who went to Vietnam and came home without a baby?"

"Yes," I replied skeptically.

"Do you have any children currently?"

"No." Where could this be going?

"Are both you and your husband Caucasian?"

Really? "Yes."

"Is your home study complete?"

"Yes." I was starting to get impatient.

Then she took a deep breath before continuing, "I had a baby born here this morning I think you might be interested in."

Stop! What? I gripped the steering wheel and took a big deep breath myself before asking her to continue.

For most of the drive home she told me the story while I tried not to swerve off the road and forced myself to watch the traffic lights and cars around me. This conversation had become very surreal.

The baby girl had been born at about 8:15 that very morning. A couple of Vietnamese descent had been driving through Oklahoma when the woman went into labor. They had lived in California but were driving across the country to visit family and eventually hoped to settle in Indiana. They were not sure when the baby was due and were surprised when the contractions started. They hadn't thought it was time yet and therefore hadn't made any plans for what would happen when the baby was born.

After the baby was born, the hospital brought in a social worker to talk with them. The couple had no insurance and currently had no jobs or home. They had no idea how they would take care of this baby, so the social worker put them in touch with Virginia's agency (Virginia was the woman on the phone). Virginia assured the couple she would find a family to adopt the child right away, with whatever characteristics they were looking for.

The couple said they wanted their daughter to be an only child, at least initially. They didn't want a family with other children to care for because they wanted to be sure she was the center of her parents' attention. They also wanted her to be adopted by a Caucasian couple. They felt it was hard to be Asian in the US, and having "a white family" would make it easier.

When families commit to an agency for domestic adoption, in addition to putting down a deposit and making a profile, the family is allowed to give parameters for the race of the child, cost of the adoption, and possible health risks that they are willing to consider. The agency then matches each birth mother with the families who meet the birth mother's requested characteristics and whose preferences also include the baby being considered.

In this case, Virginia went through their entire bank of families and didn't have a single one willing to adopt an Asian baby who fit the criteria of these birth parents—white, with no other children.

While they were scouring their database to locate such a family, the receptionist remembered talking to a lady who only wanted a baby that had already been born. That was me! I had made her listen to my whole saga of international adoption. She said this woman told a story of traveling to Vietnam—unbelievably, the same country where these parents were both born—and coming home without the baby, which necessitated starting all over.

Virginia had to go back and read the carbons from every paper message until they found the one that showed my number. The receptionist had written my information down because I insisted she keep my number "just in case."

Of course, they first began to try to reach me in mid-afternoon, just as I was getting to the barn where I had left my phone in the car.

Now I was so excited, my hands were literally shaking while I drove home, breaking all speed limits. I gave Virginia my fax number for her to send me all of the details about the birth parents and the situation. I promised I would gather some photos of myself and my husband for us to put together a make-shift portfolio to show the birth mom, and I would write her a letter. I would do all of this as soon as I got home.

I had been dealing with international adoption. Because of this, I expected I would get everything Virginia was requesting, and if everything went perfectly we might be able to go get the baby in a couple of months or so.

Once all of these logistics were discussed, Virginia asked the question I really hadn't expected. "Would you be able to get to Oklahoma to see the baby tonight?"

What? Now I had to pull over to the side of the road. Literally. Tonight? What was she talking about? I asked if I had heard her correctly as my heart was now beating louder than the voice on the phone.

It was almost 7:00 p.m. There was absolutely no way I could be in Oklahoma before midnight. Even if there was a flight that evening, I wouldn't be able to get to the airport in time for any flight before nine, and that was if I didn't do all of the paperwork or pack. Driving would take at least ten or eleven hours.

My mind was racing. Until this point, I had pretty much agreed to anything that was asked for me to do in this adoption process. But I couldn't change the laws of time and space. I had to admit there was no way I could get there.

"Well, could you be here in the morning to take the baby when she's released from the hospital?"

"Yes!" This I could manage. I could be there in the morning.

What had I just said? I would be in Oklahoma tomorrow to take a baby from the hospital? What? I couldn't even process this.

I told her I'd call back as soon as I got home, and then I hung up. By now I couldn't safely continue this conversation and focus on driving to get back to my house.

I entered the house yelling, "Marc!" He came running when he heard the urgency in my voice, and I tried to relay everything to him in one breath.

"Are you sure?" Of course Marc didn't believe I had heard this correctly. "Are you sure this isn't a scam of some sort? I don't think you can just get a baby in one day." I didn't have time to answer him just yet.

I ran upstairs and pulled the report off of the fax machine, handing it to him before reading it myself.

While he read through the report, I flipped on the computer and went straight to a travel site. I found a flight for the next morning that stopped in Dallas, but it would get me to Oklahoma City before noon. It was the only one I found that seemed reasonable, so I reserved it.

As Marc finished going through the report, he agreed it actually looked legitimate. I told him to call the agency and formally accept the referral while I ran downstairs to collect some photos. I hastily chose a few pictures of us, being sure to include at least one with the dogs and horse and a couple with our family. I got back to the office upstairs while Marc was on the phone with Virginia. We huddled around the phone, taking turns asking questions.

There was too much to ask! We didn't know where to start.

Marc asked lots of questions about the contract, finances, and commitment from all parties involved. The birth mom had twenty-four hours to make a final decision and sign away her rights. We could wire money to the agency in the morning, and it would be transferred before my flight arrived in Oklahoma City.

I asked about the baby and about the more physical logistics. The baby would be released from the hospital the next day. I would need to be there in person to sign everything at the office, but then I would take the baby to a hotel until all of the paperwork was approved by both Oklahoma and Illinois before I could leave Oklahoma. This would take about two weeks.

Finally, Virginia said she had to go home from the office and I needed to pack. I wish I could say Marc and I opened champagne and commemorated this day, but there was simply too much to do.

It was about 8:30 at night, and I literally didn't own a thing for a newborn. If we had completed one of the international adoptions, we would have brought home a baby that was no younger than six to nine months old. I had clothes, diapers and toys for a child six months and older but had never bought anything for a younger child since we didn't think we would need anything so small.

I called my sister-in-law, Joan, and filled her in as quickly as I could. She had two young children but immediately put her husband in charge and agreed to meet me at Target.

By the time we both got there, we had less than an hour before they closed. Joan took me through the whole baby section, telling me which things I would need right away and throwing all the essentials into our carts. We had filled both carts as they were announcing the store was closing.

We put everything into my car and then hugged and cried before I raced home.

Next I needed to make some reservations. I got on the computer with my credit card ready on the desk. By about 1:00 a.m. I had purchased the plane ticket I had reserved earlier, and had reserved both a hotel room and a car. Marc had dragged some suitcases from the basement, and we filled one with everything he brought up from the garage in Target bags.

Then I had to pack for myself. I had no idea where to start. I could be there for anywhere from a week to a month. And I had no idea what I would be doing while I was there!

Marc calmed me down and helped me gather piles of jeans, shorts, tops, and underwear. I threw in a couple of dresses just in case. I filled a backpack with all of the paperwork and documents I might possibly need and a folder filled with photographs of my family and of my trip to Vietnam.

We finished by 3:00 a.m., and we needed to leave for the airport by five. Marc wanted to try and sleep a little, but there was no way I could. I sat bolt upright in our bed for the next two hours and did nothing at all. My mind was filled with every thought about what could go wrong, what could go right, what would I say, and questions of whether this was all real. Before I knew what had happened, it was time to head out.

Marc assured me he would take care of things on the home front. He would find someone to take care of the dogs, talk to his boss about leaving town, get the money transferred to the agency, buy himself a ticket to join me that night, and handle anything else that may come up in the next several hours.

I was still in shock and didn't believe any of this was really happening when Marc dropped me off at O'Hare airport. I was getting on a plane to embark on this huge adventure alone, again. Although I am not very religious, I was literally praying this trip would end differently than the last one had.

Chapter 27

Ooooklahoma!

MAY, 2001

This had to be a dream. The perfect baby, of Vietnamese descent, just like we originally had our hearts set on, had just dropped out of the sky and into our laps. We could pick her up the very next day. It was obviously a dream, but I didn't want to wake up yet!

The journey to Oklahoma was a bit of a blur. I know running from one terminal to another in DFW was involved. I think there was also a delay of the second flight, but the details are scrambled in my brain. Although the trip to Vietnam had seemed last minute and frantic, I now knew that was nothing! I had a whole week to prepare for that trip. This time I had less than twelve hours. I somehow got myself a car and made my way to the adoption office at a frenetic pace.

When I got to the agency's office, no one was there. All of that rushing to arrive at an empty office? I paced back and forth and took a look around. The office was lovely and modern with Southern country decor. The walls were painted a soft soothing yellow, and bright floral curtains hung on each of the many windows. Matching spring green chairs and sofas were carefully placed around simple wooden coffee tables.

I took a seat and started flipping through a photo album filled with smiling pictures of babies in their new families. I was startled when a receptionist appeared a few minutes later, as if from nowhere. I jumped up when I heard her enter the room, spilling the album on the floor. She let me know, "Virginia just left for the hospital to get the baby discharged. Just have a seat and relax." Relax? *Really*? I didn't think that would be possible.

She handed me a huge folder of paperwork. "Just do the best you can. Virginia will help you with the rest when she gets back." More paperwork—that was no problem. I was now an expert at that.

But as I looked through the paperwork, I started having some concerns. All of our previous documentation had been prepared for an international adoption. While there were similarities, there were also some glaring differences. It was clear to me this still may not be a smooth road ahead.

One glaring discrepancy was our home study had specifically approved us for an international adoption, not a domestic one, and it appeared there may be differences in requirements for a domestic adoption, particularly from our home state of Illinois. Just as I was getting nervous about all of this, Virginia arrived back at the office with the baby and birth parents in tow.

Virginia took command of the entire space with her presence. She wasn't a large woman at all, but the confidence she exuded filled the room. She was slender, wearing a suit that was both professional and feminine, and her honey-colored wavy hair spilled over her shoulders. Her friendly face was without lines yet looked mature enough to be able to manage anything thrown at her.

Following behind her was a young Vietnamese couple in casual clothes, and the man was holding a car seat covered in a blanket.

There was that loud heartbeat again! Was this really happening? I tried to remain calm and portray the image of a perfect mother. What did that look like again? I had no idea! We all stumbled over our words a bit, but we shook hands, I peered in at the sleeping baby, and we all sat down.

The paperwork was set aside temporarily, and I was now sitting on one of the soft green sofas with the birth parents of my child sitting next to me. They looked just as exhausted as I felt and seemed to be sizing me up. They looked like a typical Vietnamese young couple, very much like all of the people in their age group I had seen in Hanoi.

The birth father was a nice-looking young man with a full head of glossy hair and appeared to be in very good shape physically. He was not tall but not unusually short, about an inch shorter than Marc. The birth mother had long thick hair that fell over her shoulders. She had lovely delicate features with a small pert nose and soulful eyes. She looked remarkably good after having given birth the previous day and even had applied some flattering makeup.

I was drawn to their faces and couldn't take my eyes off of them. I think I was hoping I could read their eyes to learn more about them. I was suddenly aware that I was staring, so I popped up and grabbed the folder I had filled with pictures from my backpack by the receptionist's desk.

First I pulled out the photos I had taken on my trip to Vietnam. Both birth parents were shocked that I had been in Hanoi! They wanted to see all the pictures and hear all of my tales. They had each come separately to the US as young teenagers with their families to seek a better life. The memories they both had of their home country were long ago but recalled fondly.

They were very surprised I had actually been *trying* to get a baby specifically from Vietnam and had even been there, but I had first-hand evidence. This shared love of their country bridged the gap a bit, and I think we all relaxed just a little.

I continued by showing them all of the family photos and describing our house and relatives. The air was charged with the heightened emotion in the room, and it was good to have something simple and concrete to focus on like our holiday cards and snapshots.

Before I felt like I was able to ask many questions of the birth parents and learn about their lives, the receptionist appeared again, saying, "It's time to go!" and herded the birth parents into her waiting car. I was left alone with Virginia, the paperwork, and the baby.

Wow! The baby! We'd almost forgotten her in all of the chaos of the three of us trying to make a good impression on the others. I picked her up from the car seat and looked into her tiny face. She was beautiful. I felt instantly drawn into her eyes as she lay in my arms.

She was pretty small, even for a newborn, at just six pounds and ten ounces. Her skin was perfectly smooth and the color of milk tea. She had big, dark-brown eyes that seemed to see me clearly, despite being only a day old, and her head was perfectly round with only the suggestion of a few tiny hairs. Just looking at her cherubic face seemed to provide a healing salve over the wounds from the other babies I had lost. I felt warm and serene as I stared at her.

I didn't have long enough to count her fingers and toes before Virginia summoned me to finish all of the documentation. I put the baby back down in the carrier and told Virginia of the discrepancies I found in the paperwork. She promised me it wouldn't be a problem.

"Home studies get amendments like these all the time," she assured me.

I wasn't totally convinced, especially after my experiences with paperwork over the last several months. But she didn't think it would require more than a simple one-paragraph addendum to the home study. We got through most of the pages and put in a call to the home study agency to request the addendum.

When the home study agency called back, the woman back in Illinois said she could write up the amendment next week but she would have to check what else would be required. She didn't know how long that would take because she didn't usually do domestic home studies, so she wasn't sure how complicated it might be to amend. Once it was complete, it could be sent down to us to be submitted to the "interstate compact" in Oklahoma for approval.

In the US every state has its own laws for adoptions. In the past, families could only adopt from the home state where they lived. But in 1960, an agreement was made that families could adopt over state lines if they abided by the laws of both states. This agreement has been in place since then, although it has been amended. Every state has its own interstate compact office that needs to approve any adoptions either originating from, or going to, that state.

So once our home study got amended properly, we could submit it to the Oklahoma compact office. They would review and ask for any additional documents or requirements to comply with Oklahoma law. If they approved it, they would send the packet up to the Illinois office to do the same. On our end, the whole thing was a waiting game.

Virginia tried to convince me all would be fine. She did this several times a month, and not only did the paperwork get approved, but the new parents quickly adapted to their roles as caretakers. I was not so sure, but I would have to figure it out.

Virginia shooed me out of the office. There was nothing more for me to do that day except get checked in at the hotel. Oh, and to learn how to take care of this baby!

Chapter 28

Vampire Baby

MAY 2001

I would love to tell a story like in a Hallmark movie where Marc and I brought the baby back to the hotel and everything was perfect. I wish I could say our first night was magical, we fell in love with this tiny precious bundle immediately, and had everything we needed to care for her at our fingertips. For me and Marc, the first night with our beautiful child felt more like being either in a horror movie or a slapstick comedy.

I packed the baby up in the car and headed to the hotel, armed with just my Target purchases and the samples of formula and other items that came in the bag from the hospital. We (new baby and I) got to the hotel and checked in. I clumsily wrangled the suitcases, backpack, and stroller, equipped with sleeping child, into the elevator and to our room.

I talked to Marc and got his airline information, learning his flight would be leaving shortly. Now I had about four hours before getting him from the airport. I would have to keep myself and this baby alive and fed for four hours with no supervision. No problem. I was an experienced mom of at least a few hours now.

The hotel room was unremarkable, clean, and modern with simple furnishings. The king bed was covered in a burgundy comforter with a pile of pillows, and a desk stood in one corner with a comfortable matching burgundy chair in the other corner. Near the bathroom was a small area with a mini fridge, sink, and coffeemaker, so we had an easy place to assemble bottles. A dark wood dresser sat across from the bed with a TV on top of it, and I began emptying the contents of one of my suitcases into it while all was quiet.

Before long the baby stirred. I took her out, changed her diaper, and fished out one of the tiny bottles from the bag. I sat peacefully in the comfy chair and stared at the tiny miracle as I fed her a bottle. *Whoah! This is what I've been fighting for this past year. It's pretty darn cute!*

I was overwhelmed by the enormity of it all. She was here. She was mine. We were a family. And I had to take care of everything this other tiny human needed for the next eighteen years. Oh my god! Marc's plane had better hurry up! I needed a partner for this job.

Once she was fed, changed, and dressed in a tiny pink outfit, I spread out a blanket on the floor and put the baby down with a pacifier.

I went to wash out the bottle and realized that our Target shopping had been far from complete. I didn't have dish soap, a sponge, or bottle brush to wash the bottle with or paper towels to dry it with.

I started taking inventory of my supplies and realized I hadn't thought of lots of other things either. I bought bottles, but they didn't have the same kinds of nipples as the ones from the hospital. The formula I picked up was a different brand too. I had gotten some clothes, but they were too big. I had diapers, but only one small package of wipes, and I'd just used four of them on a single diaper change. I had no baby shampoo or soft baby towels. Hmmm, a trip to Walmart would have to happen before we even picked up Marc.

I packed the baby back into her car seat and stuffed anything I might need into the diaper bag. I got the car seat strapped back in the car without her crying and struggled to collapse the stroller so I could stash it in the trunk.

I made my way to Walmart—fortunately right near the hotel—and put the car seat right into the shopping cart, therefore avoiding the hassle of wrestling with the stroller again. I was already learning a few tricks.

Shopping was more difficult and not as much fun as it had been with Joan, but I tried to collect all the items I had determined I would need. I took inventory of the other offerings in the infant section, trying to decide which ones would be essential while trying to remember which ones I had already purchased. I grabbed some snacks for the adults since I realized once again I had skipped eating that day and headed to the checkout. I finished just in time to get Marc from the airport.

I was pretty proud of myself. I had hunted and gathered to protect and nourish my child.

Things went pretty smoothly once we got Marc, especially given we had a day-old newborn and absolutely no preparation. As soon as Marc got into the car, we compared notes and determined we were both starving. We found a Japanese restaurant and learned they had cute little stands that held a car seat perfectly.

At dinner, I relayed the events of the day, and in doing so, we came up with several more items that I should have purchased at the store. "Babies seem to require a lot of accessories!" We wholeheartedly agreed on this point.

The three of us made our way back to Walmart after dinner and filled yet another cart with "essentials." I was getting to know the layout of Walmart and the baby department quite well. We hoped we were at least set for the night. For right now, we had a happy baby, and the two of us were managing to keep her fed, clean, and quiet.

The birth parents had named the baby Ngoc, which means Jade in Vietnamese. They told us this was a very precious stone, and she was a precious jewel to them. We agreed to keep this as one of her middle names.

I wanted to name her after my wonderful Gammy Rose, but I felt it was too soon after her death. It is traditional in the Jewish religion to name a child after a deceased loved one to honor their memory and also in hopes that the new baby will receive some of the positive qualities from their predecessor. I think I was still in a bit of denial about losing my gammy and wasn't ready to pass on her name just yet.

Marc and I agreed on Hilary, honoring both my grandfather Harry (Gammy's husband, Pop-Pop) and Marc's father Howard, both of whom had died in recent years. We hoped she would be strong and successful as both men were. We chose the middle name Elizabeth in honor of my paternal grandmother, Evelyn. We wished Hilary would develop the elegance and confidence that were Evelyn's trademarks.

Hilary Elizabeth Ngoc Asher would soon show us the stubbornness that *may* have been indicative of the family she was named for and *may* also have been a sign of who she would later become.

We got back to the hotel feeling quite accomplished. I completed what I thought would be the final feeding and changing of the night while Marc set up the Pack 'n Play crib the hotel had provided. Baby Hilary was full, drowsy, and dressed in her soft floral jammies.

After she fell asleep in my arms, I put her quietly down in the Pack 'n Play, and Marc and I whispered as we got ready for bed. Within about forty-five minutes she started to stir, and before we had even gotten across the room to peer into the crib, she was wailing and shrieking.

This was not good. We checked her diaper but it was dry as a bone. Maybe she wasn't full? We fed her again. She wouldn't drink much before her eyes started drooping. I held her a while as she drifted off to sleep again and enjoyed just watching her until I was drowsy myself. It had been quite a day!

I very gently laid her back down in her own crib without waking her and crawled under the covers. Just as I drifted off, the shrieks began again. *Again?* We repeated the same process. But no matter what we did, the sleep never lasted more than about forty-five minutes.

As we tried not to get angry at each other, Marc and I debated how early we could call the pediatrician to find out what might be wrong with our vampire baby who didn't sleep and find out how to fix it.

At about 7:00 a.m., I couldn't wait any longer! I called the doctor's office to describe the symptoms. I was sure there must be something terribly wrong. When the nurse called back, I told her the whole story and how we had tried everything! Did we need to take her to the emergency room? She was clearly quite ill or injured.

The nurse didn't seem one bit alarmed. I was sure she just wasn't understanding me. Obviously, babies were supposed to sleep for more than forty-five minutes at a time, so clearly ours was broken.

She calmly explained that Hilary had been living in a tiny space her whole life until now and the big open Pack 'n Play was scary for her. We should put her in a small bassinet.

Tears rolled down my face. "We are in a hotel room in Oklahoma," I sobbed to the nurse up in a Chicago suburb. "They don't have a bassinet here for us. We can't buy a piece of furniture and bring it back on the plane."

"It's okay," she soothed. "Do you have a car seat?"

"We do have that."

"Just strap her in there. It's cozy and safe," she suggested.

I insisted this would never work. Obviously, our baby was very sick and in need of something more than a change of environment. She assured me I could call back if she was still awake in a couple of hours.

It was magic! We strapped her in and put the car seat into the Pack 'n Play. Then we waited anxiously for her to start crying. It was thirty minutes, forty-five, sixty. How about that! Maybe the nurse knew what she was talking about after all. We closed our eyes and all actually got to sleep a few hours before she awoke again.

Our mission was almost complete. Just a few short weeks and we would be home, together as the family of three I had seen in countless dreams. This trip was thankfully nothing like the one to Vietnam. We had our baby with us and nothing else could go wrong now.

Chapter 29

Foster Parents

———

MAY 2001

I don't know why I thought the final leg of our journey would
be smoother than the rest, but the universe was having no
part of that dream. There was a difference, though. Although
there seemed to be just as many detours on our road as there
had been all along, somehow the steering was getting easier.
The obstacles resolved themselves, and I felt as if a guiding
force was helping us clear the path. Suddenly the angels were
on our side instead of working against us.

After we had all dressed and eaten breakfast on Saturday,
our first one as a family, Marc let me know he wouldn't be
able to stay in Oklahoma more than a few days. He had to get
back to Chicago for work. I started to panic a bit as I remembered the previous night and how little sleep I had gotten,
even with Marc's help. I wasn't sure I could do this all alone.

Again I thought of my very best friend, Tammy. She was
between jobs and lived in Dallas, and she wouldn't need her
passport to come to Oklahoma. She could just get in her car
and drive here!

I called and told Tammy all about Hilary. Marc and I
really hadn't spoken to anyone in the previous two days

besides my parents and Joan. It was all so surreal; we weren't sure we should tell anyone yet, but it was time to let Tammy in on our secret.

Tammy was thrilled to hear about Hilary and wanted all the details. I asked her if there was any way she could come and keep me company and help me with the baby for a few days so Marc could head back to work. I didn't mention the part that Hilary might be a vampire who only slept during the day. Being my best friend forever, Tammy jumped at the chance. "That's why we have best friends," she told me. I could breathe a sigh of relief again.

Monday was Memorial Day, so Marc and I spent the long weekend trying to learn how to take care of Hilary with few distractions. It wasn't easy, but with both of us taking turns doing the endless feeding, burping, and changing, it was pretty manageable and even enjoyable.

On Tuesday morning the peaceful path ended and detour signs started appearing again. Our home study writer called Virginia to say she had written the addendum for our report as requested, but she didn't usually do the reports for domestic adoptions. She brought it to her supervisor for review and learned the state of Illinois required adoptive parents to be licensed foster parents for domestic adoptions—an extra step that does not exist for international adoptions. Virginia didn't know about this either, as Illinois was one of very few states requiring this license.

We learned the process for becoming foster parents typically takes about six to eight weeks and includes an FBI background check and then needs to be approved by a DCFS worker. I did not want to spend the first two months with my daughter living in a hotel room!

She had already sent our paperwork to DCFS that morning, but apparently it could take several weeks just to be assigned to a DCFS case worker before the process would even begin. Our home study writer was not particularly apologetic. She repeatedly told us while writing the report that we couldn't keep changing our mind about where we were adopting from. She wasn't happy even when we switched countries and she had to make minor adjustments. Now she seemed to be getting some satisfaction in telling us, "See, you can't just do this. You needed to make a decision in the beginning and stick with it."

We got online again to learn exactly what was required. Fortunately, we had already gathered most of the paperwork we would need to become foster parents when we put together our dossiers. The biggest hurdles would be the FBI background check, getting a DCFS worker assigned to us, and then convincing that worker to expedite our case.

I called a friend who was an adoption attorney in Chicago to ask if she knew a way to speed up the process. She suggested I reach out to a government official. Marc thought this seemed far-fetched, but I figured I had little to lose.

I called the office of our local state representative with limited expectations. The young man who answered the phone was the representative's assistant. He was enthusiastic and new to the job, telling me he wanted to help.

"Our problem is not a simple one," I began.

"That's okay. How can I help?" He was undeterred by my pessimism.

I poured out the details, recounting the story of my trip to Vietnam and how everything went wrong, the journey with all of the different countries, and ended with how the universe led us to this Vietnamese baby in Oklahoma, but then we didn't have the right kind of home study. He and I were both tearful by the time I reached the end of our story, and he was determined to help us get home.

Together we made up a game plan. I would do what I could to get the FBI clearances taken care of, and my new friend was going to tackle the DCFS office. He promised to reach back out to me by the end of the day to compare notes.

The supervisor at the home study office explained that we needed to get fingerprinted at a specific office for the FBI clearance, which was in Chicago. She told me I would have to fly home to get this done and I would need an appointment. Marc would have to get his done whenever he could get the first appointment, and then I would have to fly up whenever the next appointment was available. Per the interstate compact agreement, Hilary wasn't allowed to leave the state of Oklahoma until everything had been approved by both Oklahoma and Illinois. I couldn't leave Hilary alone, and Marc had to get back to work. I told her we would find another way.

I scoured the internet trying to find clarification or options for the fingerprint requirement. Eventually I called the FBI directly and got someone on the phone who said the only other way to get the clearance was to get manual ink fingerprints taken, and not many places did those any more. I would have to find a police station that would be willing to take our prints on the FBI cards, which they could send to me. I paid to have one set of the FBI cards sent overnight to my hotel and another sent to my house in Illinois. Then I set my mind to finding the right police station.

I called several police stations near the hotel, but they were all unwilling or unable to help us. After many calls, I finally found a kind officer who told me he could do it for me. I made an appointment for the following afternoon since I needed to wait for the cards to be delivered.

Marc was flying home the next morning, so he would have to find a place to get his prints done up in Chicago. One of us would make the calls to find a willing policeman in Chicago once he was up there. I needed to tackle just one thing at a time.

Just before five, my friend from the representative's office called me back. He had spent most of the day on my case, calling everyone he could find at DCFS. He hadn't quite gotten it taken care of yet, but he would. He left a message for the head of the whole agency, with specific reference to the state representative. He knew the DCFS office depended upon state funding and was confident he would get a return call in the morning. "Keep your chin up!" he told me. "We're going to make this happen." I felt as if he had been sent to me straight from heaven.

The next morning, which was Wednesday, I dropped Marc at the airport, made yet another trip to Walmart to refill some of our provisions, and headed back to the hotel to gather my express package from the FBI. It was waiting for me at the front desk, and I turned right around and left for my appointment at the police station.

The officer I met with explained that most stations wouldn't do ink prints anymore. They had their own internal electric systems now, but he still had the supplies to get mine done. A female officer played with Hilary while I rolled each finger in ink.

I explained more of the story, and the compassionate police captain said he had a friend up north who might be able to help Marc. I took his phone number and filed it in my purse.

Marc landed that afternoon back in Chicago and started calling stations with no luck. On my way back to the hotel I called and gave Marc the number from the card in my purse.

Marc couldn't believe it. After all the calls he had made, it was like magic; the policeman in a neighboring suburb to ours who answered from that number told Marc he would do the prints for him. We both got them sent out by overnight mail for our clearances.

Just before five, again, I heard from my young government friend. He told me he had been thinking about me all day but wanted to have good news when he called. He had just finally heard back from the head of DCFS, and the top caseworker had been assigned to our family. She would call us first thing in the morning.

He also asked me to send him an email describing the whole situation so he would be able to justify the time he had spent to his boss. I was more than happy to comply. He'd spent the better part of two days doing this for me. Anything I could do to help him, I would get done in a heartbeat.

Tammy drove up from Dallas and arrived that evening despite the first of many thunderstorms that week. We learned Oklahoma gets storms that are more violent and more frequent than we saw in Illinois. Tammy was a little soggy when she got to our room, but I was so happy to see her!

We ordered food, and I told her about everything going on while we played with and admired beautiful Hilary. I had asked her to come that evening because Hilary had her first pediatrician's appointment the following morning and I wanted someone to be with me.

There may have been a tornado warning outside, but in our hotel room, this fun night with just the three girls was the beautiful calm before our next storm.

Chapter 30

BFF

———

Nothing is more valuable than a best friend.

Thursday morning we arrived on time to the pediatrician's office, but they hadn't received Hilary's records from the hospital. This doctor was Virginia's personal pediatrician, so they called over to Virginia to ask her to get in touch with the hospital and have the information we needed faxed over right away.

While we waited, we got the baby's exam done, and all looked good. She, in fact, did have ten fingers and toes and had even gained a few ounces in her first week of life. Just as we were finishing the exam, the nurse came in holding a faxed report with a worried look on her face.

The hospital hadn't gotten the blood work processed for Hilary's birth mom before she left, and they had no way to reach her once the results were processed. Her birth mom had tested positive for Hepatitis B, the same disorder that had ruled out baby Viet in Vietnam. I started to panic again.

The doctor told me to calm down. A vaccination could be given to babies called an H-Big shot. It was unlikely the baby would have already developed the disease, and this vaccine kept it from infecting her. Oh, that was great! Just give her the vaccine.

"Well, it's not that easy," the pediatrician explained. "This vaccine is very new and is regulated by the government. They keep all doses in Washington, DC, and send it out to Hep B positive pregnant women about a month before their due date so it can be given at birth." I smiled and nodded at the doctor. No problem, we would have a dose sent from Washington. I was happy to pay the FedEx fees.

The doctor continued to explain, "It is only approved to be given until the baby is seven days old."

It was Thursday. Hilary was born the prior Thursday. She was seven days old today. Today was the last day she could get the shot!

While I was doing mental gymnastics trying to wrap my head around all of this, the doctor left and came back with a folder. She had a patient who was Hep B positive delivering soon and actually had her dose of H-Big waiting at the hospital. The patient had enough time to get another dose shipped from Washington, but she would have to give her permission to relinquish this dose.

The doctor asked Tammy to take Hilary down to the lab for a special blood test that would confirm she was negative for Hep B right now. I should wait for the other patient's approval because I would need to race over to the hospital to retrieve the precious vaccine so it could be administered to Hilary before the end of the day.

Tammy got directions to the lab downstairs, packed up Hilary and her diaper bag, and headed to the elevator. I waited around just a few minutes while the receptionist called each of the numbers from the chart of the pregnant patient.

We got the permission (I was going to need to send a fruit basket to all of these people) and I sped across town to the hospital. I had to explain my whole story to several secretaries, nurses, and receptionists before locating the tiny vial. I tucked the precious cargo into my purse and hurried back to the doctor's office.

When I got back to the pediatrician's I was horrified to find both Tammy and Hilary covered in blood. "She's your baby alright!" Tammy sighed. "She screamed and kicked the whole time. We needed three nurses to help get her blood drawn." They both looked weary from the battle.

We didn't lose any time preparing for another fight. I held Hilary's tiny arms and Tammy pinned her little legs while the nurse gave her the vaccine.

"I thought this was going to be easy," Tammy said when we got in the car.

I had a message from the DCFS worker on my phone that I hadn't noticed during our most recent crisis. I didn't even respond to Tammy before opening my phone. I called her back and was pleasantly surprised.

"I've been assigned to your case and was told to approve it as soon as your FBI clearance comes through," she told me immediately. "You must have friends in very high places. Usually it takes weeks to get assigned a worker at all, and I don't take on many cases since I'm the supervisor. But it looks like all of your other paperwork is in order."

"I sure do!" I confirmed. My new friend at the representative's office had certainly done his best for us!

The DCFS supervisor said she was on top of it and would call us as soon as she heard from the FBI.

Virginia had gotten the amended home study report—minus the foster care approval—on Tuesday and sent all of our paperwork to the interstate compact office in Oklahoma. She left a message for me while we were busy waging war on the infant at the doctor. Oklahoma had approved everything since they didn't require the foster care license for adoptions. They had sent our packet overnight express to the Illinois interstate compact office, and it would be there first thing in the morning. That was quick! The boxes were all getting checked off.

Tammy and I got to spend the next day playing with the baby and making yet another trip to Walmart for some new clothes. I cherished this time with my best friend. Only the most special person would have been there for me the way she was. I am so grateful to have her.

Tammy had been a very special friend for many years. I had hoped she would have been able to join me in Vietnam, but since she hadn't, I was glad to have her with me in Oklahoma. I mentioned that Tammy and I met in middle school and we became best friends on the very first day we met. This instant connection is extremely rare, especially between middle school girls. I had missed my bus on that day early in our seventh grade year, and Tammy invited me to take her bus and come over to her house. Together we forged a note from my mom to get on her bus, and the rest is kind of history.

We were best friends from that day on. We were completely inseparable in high school and spent several nights a week together alternating sleeping at the other's house. We ate lunch together at school each day and spent hours on the phone when we weren't together. We both felt fully a part of the other's family, and she is the closest thing to a sister I will ever have.

Although Tammy and I didn't take the same path in life after high school, we were always still there for the other. We went to colleges on different ends of the country, but she came to visit me in Philly and I spent some fun days with her in California. She was the maid of honor at my wedding, and I was the only person to stand up in hers.

The importance of my best friend has continued to the current day. Although she isn't Jewish, Tammy was called to the altar thirteen years after Hilary's birth to be honored at her bat mitzvah. When Tammy's father died, I flew down to her immediately and helped her write the eulogy.

Now, like usual on momentous occasions, we were back together. Not only were we getting to spend precious time together, but Tammy was the first one (besides Marc) I introduced to my daughter. We got to have some "girl time" between the three of us. We shopped for super cute girly clothes for Hilary and went out for dinner. We talked and talked and talked.

We had the delicious opportunity to spend time together with no real distractions, just catching up. This girl time added my brand-new daughter to a bond that is stronger than steel and more precious to me than diamonds. I will always remember and cherish that day and the place it solidified for Tammy in Hilary's life.

It was hard to say goodbye the next morning. Reconnecting in such an intense situation had deepened our friendship as adults. It was a privilege to have Tammy's help, companionship, and the opportunity to confide in someone I truly trusted about the insecurities of being a new mom. But Marc was coming back that afternoon, and Tammy was looking forward to having the weekend with her boyfriend back home. It was time for her to go. We hugged as she got into her car to head home, and I left to pick up Marc at the airport.

Best friends are amazing, and I treasure this time I spent with Tammy. She was also so much help, but in the end, I knew this baby was my job. It was time to have my partner back to share this responsibility. A new baby is a lot of work, and things are definitely easier with both parents together.

Chapter 31

There's No Place Like Home!

JUNE 2001

We had our daughter in our arms, and nothing would keep us from bringing her home. We just had to get through a night of lightning, hail, and tornadoes first.

The thunderstorms had continued each night since Tammy arrived on Wednesday. It was now Saturday, and a storm was raging yet again. Marc's flight landed on time despite the weather, and I breathed a sigh of relief when I saw him come out of the airport. I was so glad to have him back.

We picked up dinner and barely made it back to the hotel room before a tornado warning was issued. We turned on the TV to watch the weather report, but within an hour the screen turned black because the hotel had lost power. The emergency lights went on in the hallway, so we kept our door open to have light for dinner. Then we all went to bed early and fell asleep easily with the sounds of the pelting rain and howling wind just outside our window.

About 2:00 a.m. we were awakened by Hilary's wails. We both jumped up from our sleep, but it was completely pitch black. The power was still out, and I couldn't see a thing because the emergency lights were off now too. My first thought was to rush to the baby, but as soon as my feet hit the floor, I ran into something and stubbed my toe. I sat back down on the bed. I couldn't even get to the baby without tripping over something. My toe was hurting so I yelled, "Ma-arc!" in a whiny voice.

"Let me get my phone," he replied. He hadn't wanted to use it earlier because we didn't have any way to charge it and mine had already died. It had about 20 percent power left, but just refreshing the screen made it shine with a dim glow.

We had just enough light from the screen to barely see what we were doing. I held the phone inches away from the baby while Marc managed to change her dirty diaper. Marc still counts this as one of his most heroic acts of fatherhood.

After we got Hilary settled back to sleep, Marc and I turned to each other in the darkness and giggled. "After what we've been through, no little tornado is going to faze us," I whispered to my husband. I had to pinch myself to believe we were really all together.

The storms died down and power was restored by the time we woke up on Sunday. We tried to make plans, not knowing how long it would be before we could go home. But it was okay. We had gotten this far, and I was sure we must be at the end of our quest. We agreed to just wait another day before planning anything and see what would happen on Monday.

Since we'd gotten to Oklahoma, everything seemed to be falling in place. Although crazy potholes in our metaphorical road appeared from nowhere, we had an incredible team of angels here—Virginia, Tammy, the Illinois State representative and her assistant, the police officer, the pediatrician, and an anonymous Hep B positive mother—who filled in each hole as it came up.

We still didn't know what our immediate future would look like. Marc couldn't stay down with me much longer, and we had no way to know when the foster care license would be issued so we could take Hilary out of Oklahoma. We knew we had only a few days before we would have logistics to handle again. I don't know why, but I wasn't worried. I could just feel somehow that it was all going to be okay.

I was right. Everything was on track. On Monday morning I was woken up by the sound of my phone ringing. It was the call we were waiting for. On the phone was our incredulous DCFS agent. She got a message as soon as she got in to the office from the FBI granting our clearance. She was signing off on our case after just two business days, the fastest she had ever done. She was submitting our approval that day, and we were free to travel at our leisure. I added her to our list of angels.

I started to laugh. I'm not sure why, but I laughed so hard I cried. Marc got on the phone and thanked the woman profusely since I could no longer speak through the tears.

All that had happened hit me during that call, and I couldn't stop crying. Just fourteen months before this day, Marc and I had agreed to have a child.

We spent about eight months enduring two miscarriages. For many couples, this might have been the end of their search for a child, but we were undeterred.

We began our adoption quest in November, just six months prior. Since then, we'd lived through many months of tedium. We learned all we could about adoption in general and about several foreign countries. We got to know and work with several different adoption agencies. We collected more paperwork than we ever thought would be needed for anything.

I left my tranquil life and home for a week to take a voyage to the other side of the earth. While I was there, we had challenges we never could have imagined. Each time one problem emerged, it led to a tangle of other problems, and everything fell apart around us. I left a piece of my heart there in Vietnam, in the hands of a beautiful little infant girl. I was able to get myself back around the globe, but the challenges didn't end there.

We started over and began the process for six different possible international adoptions. Each time we stumbled but got ourselves back up. We dutifully continued to research and file paperwork until we got a call from the Sooner state and headed south the very next day.

We'd spent the last week and a half in Oklahoma, where roadblocks continued to emerge. Fortunately, this trip was not the same as the one to Vietnam. In just ten short days we conquered concerns from the FBI clearances, foster care licensure, Hepatitis, and even tornadoes. Unlike in Vietnam, this child was meant to be ours, so we were able to resolve each of these issues instead of them leading to more problems.

This had been the hardest year of my life. My spirit had lost two babies to miscarriage, one to international adoption, and my dear Gammy to infection, but my soul was now at peace.

All that Marc and I witnessed and experienced had culminated in this tiny, perfect being. It was time to bring her home.

I went downstairs to the hotel computer and booked a flight home for that very evening and then spent the rest of the day making phone calls. I called the home study worker and Virginia to let them know we were cleared. I called the office of the State Representative and talked to my now dear friend, thanking him for all he had done to bring us home. I called my parents, Tammy, Micki, and Joan. I told everyone our journey was complete and we would be back in Illinois that night.

I had Marc with me to pack everything up and say good-bye to Oklahoma, and I was so glad. We were making the return trip together—unlike all of the flights we had gotten used to taking in the past year alone.

We got to come back to our own house together as a new family of three. Our beautiful baby girl was happy, healthy, and ours. She was the perfect fit for us. She needed us, and we needed her. She was the "right" baby, and from that day on I can't even imagine our lives without her.

Afterword

———

Hilary has truly been a miracle in our lives. She fit right in with us, and it was always clear from the moment we met her that she was supposed to be our daughter.

Right after we got home from Oklahoma, an article was published about us in the local paper. The man at the state representative's office had forwarded the email of my story along with updates about how the representative had helped us get home to a reporter who published the story.

While we were living it, I don't think Marc and I were completely aware of how bizarre and extraordinary our journey had been, but my friend was taken by the story. He was sure the audience of the paper would want to read about our adoption quest and its storybook ending.

Hilary completed our family and filled a hole in my soul that I hadn't known was there. In less than two years, she made it clear to us that our family was not yet complete, though. She wanted a brother or sister.

We adopted a little boy, Jamie, when Hilary was about two and a half, and then two years later I gave birth to a biological son, Reese (named for my dear Gammy Rose). Each of the three of them was a miracle for us. Each has their own very different story of joining our family, and I believe the five of us were destined to be together, despite our many differences.

I have definitely met my match with my gorgeous daughter. Hilary is a constant challenge but also my greatest joy. She has kept me on my toes since she was a day old and continues to do so every day, twenty years later.

Although I had my heart set on Hilary riding and showing horses with me, she had other plans. She had no interest in the adorable pony I bought her when she was just eighteen months old. She picked her own way in the world and was drawn to the ice from the age of five. She became a competitive figure skater, a sport I have always enjoyed watching, and is still competing at a high level at the time of this book's publication.

It has been very healthy for us to each have our own sport. We have something we excel at and can also enjoy teaching the other.

I learned to skate a little when Hilary was in grade school, and Hilary has taught me more than I could ever do on ice when I took lessons as a child. I love living for a moment on her blades, in her world. I also have learned so much about the sport being her manager and advocate for many years.

She learned to ride horses, too, and even spent one summer joining me on my equestrian drill team.

It is hard to explain in words how Hilary is a perfect match for our family, but it is often pointed out to me by people we know, including friends, family, and even strangers who spend a short time with us.

The baby I fell in love with in Vietnam also found her perfect family. When I was involved in the online group of families adopting from Vietnam, I was able to locate her. I was telling another mom about my trip and the orphanage

I visited. We exchanged photos and saw that we had been to the same exact place. She was in Vietnam with the family who adopted that baby.

"My" baby in Thai Nguyen was adopted by an incredible couple in Canada. They are her perfect match, and she has grown into a lovely young woman. Hilary was able to meet her when we were on an unexpected trip near her hometown. We'd had very little contact up to that point, and we were all nervous about this impromptu meeting. It had been fourteen years since I saw that tiny baby in the basket at the orphanage.

As soon as the girls saw each other across the parking lot, they ran toward each other as if they were in a movie. Between the two moms and the two girls, a whole lot of happy tears were shed that day. I felt such peace in seeing personally that "my" baby had such a wonderful life.

Her real mom and dad had very little information about the early months of her life. They have never met their daughter's birth mom, and the information they got from Vietnam was very limited. I was basically the first person her mom got to talk to who knew her daughter before she did and could fill in some tiny portions of her story before adoption.

The girls saw a sister in each other. Neither one grew up with a sister, and they had both always yearned for one. They still keep in touch and feel a close bond despite many miles between them.

The two women I traveled to Vietnam with also adopted children. Pat adopted a little girl, although I don't know where she was adopted from. Jan adopted a beautiful little boy from Cambodia. We kept in touch for many years and still exchange holiday cards.

After my sons were born, I was so grateful for my children that I wanted to work in the adoption field. I felt lucky and blessed to have the opportunity to raise these amazing kids, and I wanted to help other families to find the children meant for them. I also hoped I could help them to avoid some of the pain, stress, and pitfalls I had experienced in my journey. I had the privilege of working with many families and feel lucky to still call some of them my friends.

I worked at first as a birth mother counselor, helping birth moms make a decision about what would be best for themselves and their children. I then worked as an adoption consultant helping adoptive families—at first for a firm with several consultants who counseled families through the domestic adoption process. Later I started my own company doing the same work. I did this work for several years and knew of a large number of families who found their children through adoption. Some were my clients and others were clients of my colleagues who I worked with collaboratively.

In all the years I worked with families, I have yet to hear of another family who adopted a Vietnamese child in the US. In this country, it is typical in the Vietnamese culture for extended family members to raise a child whose parents are unable to care for him or her. In fact, we later learned this had happened even with Hilary's birth parents. Hilary has an older biological brother and sister. When her pregnant birth mom left California, she left her older two children in the care of her mother and sister. These siblings were raised by their aunt for many years on and off until their mother was in a situation stable enough to keep them herself.

I feel like the fact that Hilary is Vietnamese, after everything I went through in Vietnam, was a sign to us she was meant for our family.

The adoption process can be frustrating, tedious, and lonely. Often one of my client families would struggle, waiting for everything to fall into place. While I truly believe that children find their correct family, it can be difficult to understand and believe this when families are in the depths of the adoption process.

Sometimes parents are so eager they have a hard time waiting, like I did. When this happened with my clients, I told them the story of my adoption and how I pushed so hard as everything kept falling apart around me. Each time I tried to find a loophole or rush through a step of the adoption process, something went terribly wrong.

No matter how hard I tried, I couldn't rush the journey. I could only make the process more frenetic, but it wouldn't cause my daughter to be born any sooner. The universe had to stall me and kill time before it was able to bring me together with my baby girl, and no amount of manipulation on my part could make that happen before the time was right. In sharing my story I like to think I helped to make that waiting period a little easier to endure.

Several clients encouraged me to publish this very story, but for many years it was too emotional for me to put out into the world. I am sharing this story now publicly in hopes of helping other parents stay faithful and to encourage their belief in the adoption process and that all things happen as they are supposed to.

I learned a lot during the time I was waiting for Hilary. Through my research and travel, I fell in love with the Vietnamese culture and people. I thought they were the most beautiful children I had ever seen, and the culture was not only lovely but warm and welcoming.

Many of my client families found my story meaningful, powerful, and inspirational. Some even told me it gave them the strength and courage to move forward as well as faith that their correct child would come into their life when the time was right.

Time and again my faith was tested and restored. I saw so many incredible stories that clearly illustrated children coming to the families who were perfectly, uniquely suited to their specific, ideally matched baby. In fact, still years later, I will see a story on Facebook posted by a former client. Some quality or talent will have emerged within their child that shows or reinforces just how much they are meant to be in their special family.

One of the clearest and most dramatic situations is so beautiful I want to share it. These clients were one of the most physically attractive couples I have ever worked with. They literally look like a modern Barbie and Ken. I helped them find their first son, a stunningly beautiful child they adopted at birth.

When this family decided their son needed a sibling, they called me again to help them find their second child.

This client's scrapbook made for birth moms was so beautiful I used it as an example for many other families. They were not just gorgeous, but they were both educated, successful professionals. They had designed and built their dream home, which looked like a giant lodge. They are adventurous and outdoorsy, and their book is full of photos of them biking, hiking, and on the beach during their regular vacations to Aruba.

I thought every single birth mom who got to see this book would choose them instantly. I mean, I wanted them to adopt *me*! But that didn't happen. In several situations where the family was really excited about a birth mom, they were skipped over for a different family.

During their process, they were chosen by more than one birth mom, but the situations kept falling apart for one reason or another. Eventually they were matched with a birth mom they adored and who seemed very invested in them as well.

They were matched for several months and became extremely attached. Then one day the birth mom just disappeared. She stopped responding to the family and wasn't even in touch with the agency. After a huge number of attempts to reach her, we all had to accept that she was gone and the family was back to square one.

While I truly believe there is a plan for all of us, the universe was really testing my faith here. This wonderful family didn't deserve this kind of heartbreak. It had been a year since they called me to help them, and I had never had a client wait that long to be matched.

But as soon as my faith was tested, it was just as quickly restored and reinforced. A couple of weeks later, my clients called me excited and breathless. "We got a call from our son's birth mom," they told me. "She is having another baby in just a couple of weeks, and she wants him to be raised in our family with his biological brother!"

Now, imagine if one of those other situations had worked out. My clients would have a toddler and a newborn and would be faced with quite a difficult decision. The universe just needed them to wait for their second son to be ready for them.

You couldn't have told me this at the time, but I needed to live through every heartbreak and annoyance I experienced. I'm now glad for everything I went through. Without that frightening and frenetic trip to Vietnam, I would probably never have the deep knowledge and appreciation of my daughter's culture of birth as I do now. I also may not have had the same bond with her birth parents without that trip.

Additionally, making this trip alone greatly boosted my own self-confidence and helped me tackle many fears about traveling by myself.

I was able to see the beautiful babies at the orphanage in Thai Nguyen and tell one adoptive mom more about her daughter's history. I was able to see the nightlife of Hanoi that I likely never would have observed if everything had gone as planned.

I believe learning about the other countries deepened my love for the Vietnamese culture as well.

Gathering all of the endless paperwork gave me perspective on what is required of orphanages and adoption agencies to fulfill the requirements of the government.

Jumping through the hurdles in Oklahoma made me appreciate the challenges of domestic adoption and also helped to solidify the bond between me and Hilary.

I am grateful for everything I went through and also for the wisdom it gave me to be able to help other families.

Over all, I wouldn't change a thing and will always feel lucky to have embarked upon this journey.

I hope that reading this story has helped you to have faith in the universe. I believe there is a plan for all of us and that we need to be open to seeing the signs showing us the right direction. Everyone's signs are different, and only you can recognize what feels right. The path won't always be easy but the lessons of the journey will feed our souls. I am grateful every day that I was able to have the patience (barely) to follow my own path to my daughter. My daughter and sons are my inspiration and my greatest joy. Our journey continues together as a family.

Acknowledgments

———

I would like to acknowledge first my family who tolerated me while working on this project. My husband, Marc, who left me alone when I couldn't pull myself away from the computer and even helped me create a warm office space where I could write. My children, Hilary, James, and Reese, who have given me the best job of my life—being a mom. You are my world. Also my parents, Michael and Ann Rosenblum, who always helped me believe I can do anything I decide to do. Thank you to my late grandparents, Rose and Harry Baseman and Evelyn and Jacob Rosenblum, who not only raised my parents but who always loved me just for existing.

Thank you to my guides on this original journey and dear friends, Micki Elmer and Virginia Frank, without whom this would definitely not be the story it is.

Thank you to my amazing tribe of friends who are way too numerous to list, but especially Tammy Oei Adams, who has been as constant in my life as any member of my family.

Thank you to everyone who supported my book:

Ann Rosenblum

Sheryl Abrams Gilman

Tony Slevira

Joan and Robert Asher

Kelly Fitzhugh

Christie Lane

Shirley and Pat Keating

Nancy Bates

Sean and Michelle Murphy

Rachel and Earl Bloom

April Evans

Amy Matz

Ira Letofsky

Suzanne Swain

Carol Margolis

Ellen and Donny Baseman

Lisa Smith

Eric Koester

Susan Widenbaum Vainik

Rhonda Arza

Jeff Rosenblum

Molly Bonney

Lisa and Aaron Brooks

Rachel Schick Siegel

Betty Ballard

Amy Davidson

James Kargman

Lauren Ciarochi

Susan Addelson

Jeanne Koepke

Beth Vicano

Dana Freed

Laurie K. Weiss

Jennifer Blice

Stacey Finster

Sue Schroeder

Susan Fried

Rachel Friem

Marla Parvey

Betsy Rubin

Carrie Wall

Lisa Olschwanger

Nora Hansen

Ella Epshteyn

Maya Simon

Amy Conway-Hatcher

Paula Sotelo

Warren Packard

Helen Katsman

Adrienne Bransky

Anna Gabelev

Virginia Frank

Adoption Choices of Kansas

Angela Baseman

Breelie Taylor

Sheila Paige

Winnie Robie

Kristi Udell

Lilli Erickson

Janet Barton

Julie Godnik

Michelle Matias

Donna and David Tropp
Maryann Lombardi
Heather Shapan
Ella Rasin
Harrison Wein
Helen Rosenblum
Jennifer Coppess
Suzanne Hales
Anne Pekoske
Richard and Susan Baseman
Gina Rubel
Kelly M. Killeen
Beth Dorman
Steven Lefton Sharp
Aaron Woolfson
Erika Boylan
JoAnn Farris
Robert James
Deborah Conner
Erik Santiago
Robert Mansur
Karline Peal
Klee Hartfield
Stephanie Orsi
Suzanne Bender-Van Spyk
Tammy and Ken Adams
Kimberly Friedman
Doris Bonvino
April Walker
Susan Pristave

Steven Hummel
Corrie Shores
Pierre Panayi
Steven Ginsburg
Hilary Valente
Rebecca Chinery-Karnes
Lee Schild
Mary Tyree
Jennifer Conrad
Tejal Thakur
Sheila Goldberg
Joe Alter
Jennifer Matthews-Pate
Gisele Frantz
Barbara Kavanagh
Cindy Ray Yablonsky
Marc R Lawrence
Margie Rolston
Holly Tomlin
Jaynee Buss
Micki Elmer
MariAnn Gattelaro
Shysel Granados
Mercedes Thorne
Cory Sureck
Barb Pagano
Sandra James
Joseph Buckland
Lisa Schaefer
Melanie Heaney

Karen Richards	Dawn Niebel
Amy Young	Susan Packard
Sheila Lonergan	Jonathan Marguiles
Andrew Davidson	Mickael Krizmanic
Chika Sekiguchi	

I would also like to thank Rob Asher for his design expertise and help with my graphics and cover art. Further, thank you to the group of beta readers who read my early manuscripts and gave me feedback on my writing.

Ann Rosenblum	Micki Elmer
Richie Baseman	Charis Negley
Joan Asher	Steven T. Ginsburg
Cory Sureck	

Special thanks goes out to everyone at the Creator Institute at Georgetown University and at New Degree Press. In particular to Eric Koester, Brian Bies, Jordana Megonigal, Shawna Quigley, Jessica Drake-Thomas, Amanda Brown, Steven Howard, John Saunders, and Kyra Dawkins. Thank you all for putting up with me, even when I had unending questions and was unnecessarily needy.

I am finally very grateful to the furry members of my life who have kept my mind clear and my heart full, especially Tinkerbell, Buddy, Furgie, and Dolly.

Jennifer Rose Asher is the author of *Journey to My Daughter*. This memoir is her first book and details her journey of miscarriage, adoption and self-discovery. Jennifer has a Master's degree in counseling psychology and worked in the adoption field for several years before documenting her own story. Jennifer lives in the Dallas area with her husband and three children, two of whom joined her family through adoption. She also shares her life with four beloved dogs and two quarter horses.

Appendix

CHAPTER 8

Adoption Network. "US Adoption Statistics." Adoptionnetwork. com. Last modified 2021. https://adoptionnetwork.com/adoption-myths-facts/domestic-us-statistics/.

CHAPTER 25

Miller, Laurie, Wilma Chan, Aina Litvinova, Rubin Arkady, Kathleen Comfort, Linda Tirella, Sharon Cermak, Barbara Morse, and Igor Kovalev. "Fetal Alcohol Spectrum Disorders in Children Residing in Russian Orphanages: A Phenotypic Survey." *Alcoholism, Clinical and Experimental Research.* 30, no. 3. (April 2006): 531-8. doi:10.1111/j.1530-0277.2006.00059.x